the
darwin Awards

the
darwinĀwar̆ḑs

INTELLIGENT DESIGN

Wendy Northcutt

with Christopher M. Kelly

This edition first published by
Orion Books
an imprint of the Orion Publishing Group Ltd
Orion House, 5 Upper St Martin's Lane,
London WC2H 9EA

First published in hardback in the USA by Dutton,
an imprint of Penguin Group (USA) Inc.

A CIP catalogue record for this book is available
from the British Library.

ISBN-13: 978 0 75287 562 0
ISBN-10: 0 75287 562 0

Printed in Great Britain by Clays Ltd, St Ives plc

The Orion Publishing Group's policy is to use papers that are natural, renewable
and recyclable and made from wood grown in sustainable forests. The logging and
manufacturing processes are expected to conform to the environmental regulations
of the country of origin.

www.orionbooks.co.uk

This one's for you, babe.*

*Homage to Christine Lavin's song, "Don't Ever Call Your Sweetheart by His Name"

If all else fails, immortality
can always be assured
by spectacular error.

—John Kenneth Galbraith

Contents

Motorcycles, trucks, trains, cars, snowmobiles, mopeds, a wheelchair, and one mountain bike—wheels spark a powerful urge to test mechanical limits. The stories in this chapter show that humans still have a long way to go, in evolving to cope with the ubiquitous dangers of our transportation system.

CHAPTER 2
Water   65

*Water covers 70 percent of the Earth's surface, so it's little won-
der that this is the medium in which many Darwin demises occur. We herein encounter the dangers of "snowmoboating," the*

tide, frozen rivers, raging rivers, two waterfalls, one bungee cord, and even the kitchen sink! Dive into stories featuring water, where one soon sees that our evolutionary adaptations are not yet complete.

CHAPTER 3
Women   **89**

Few women win Darwin Awards, but this book is lucky enough to have a strong selection of female applicants. We have a spy, two explosions, pilot sex and street sex, a desperate smoker, a gymnast, an amateur mechanic, and a thief. We also have a Jet Ski, a hurricane, a raging river, a roller coaster, gasoline, and an aerosol can. It is with great pleasure that I introduce these stories about feminine wiles. . . .

CHAPTER 4
Animals   **117**

An animal might win a Darwin Award if it migrated in the wrong direction. But in this chapter, animals are not the winners; they are the backdrop against which humans lose to Mother Nature. Enjoy these stories about elephants, snakes, raccoons, chickens, bees, bugs, birds, eels, sharks, toads, horses, and bison—animals that have the misfortune to share the planet with clueless Homo sapiens.

CHAPTER 5
Alcohol   **149**

Alcohol plays a role in many Darwin Awards, but this is the first chapter devoted exclusively to the boneheaded things we do while inebriated. Get ready for a spy device, freeway calisthenics, saliva, bar bets, sunglasses, revenge, a beer-filled condom, window glass, a drinking glass, auto repair, firecrackers, and a submarine. Here are stories of inebriated innovations that make mice and monkeys cringe when we say we're related to them. . . .

CHAPTER 6
Explosion/Fire   181

Pyrotechnics aren't just for professionals; amateurs frequently find the allure of explosives too great to pass up. With grenades, bombs, dynamite, gasoline, a mine detonator, electricity, ammunition, acetylene, chemicals, methane, lots of fireworks, a fire-breather, a bungee cord, and even a lava lamp, there's never a shortage of examples for fire-safety courses!

CHAPTER 7
Weapons   **225**

Whether wielded on the right side of the law, the wrong side, or no side of the law at all, weapons tend to bite the hand that feeds them. Guns, grenades, knives, bullets, and axes all hold a grudge against those who abuse them. In the following stories, misused weapons themselves act as judge and jury to mete out their own form of justice. . . .

CHAPTER 8
Miscellaneous   **249**

Some innovative Darwin Awards don't fall into predictable categories. Enjoy the miscellaneous methods man has invented to bedevil himself, using thallium, an ice maker, trees, scaffolding, a confession, a nail gun, a homemade parachute, chocolate sauce, eletromagnets, an innocent paper-towel dispenser, and an auger—two different ways. They are all examples that one

*should avoid emulating, if one wants to keep the body's me-
tabolism running efficiently—or running at all!*

Introduction

The title, *Darwin Awards 4: Intelligent Design,* pokes fun at the embarrassing pseudo-science of religious fundamentalists. True intelligent design is the unerring scythe of natural selection.

WHAT, ME WORRY?
WHY THERE ARE DARWIN AWARDS

The role model for the Darwin Awards is Wile E. Coyote, whose relentless pursuit of Road Runner leads him to find creative solutions to nonexistent problems, none of which work the way he planned. True Darwin Award candidates imagine that they live in a world where tigers don't bite, sharks are as cuddly as stuffed animals,[1] and people can fly with a little ingenuity.[2] In their minds, steering a motorcycle with their feet just makes sense.[3] In their world, it's easy to go to the chopping block and confuse a private body part with a chicken neck.[4]

Benjamin Franklin once said, "We are all born ignorant, but one must work hard to remain stupid." Darwin Awards celebrate those who work the hardest. By removing themselves from the gene pool, they give their all for the good of the rest of us. To paraphrase Neil Armstrong, "That's one small misstep for man, one giant leap for mankind."

Most of us know instinctively that the phrase "trust me, light this fuse" is a recipe for disaster. Darwin Award winners do not. Most of us have a basic common sense that eliminates

[1] WADES WITH SHARKS, page 139
[2] ICARUS, page 274
[3] DARING FEET, page 30
[4] CHICKEN TO GO, page 129

the need for NO SMOKING signs at gas stations. Darwin Award winners do not. No warning label could have prevented evolution from creeping up on the homeowner who filled his house with natural gas to kill termites,[4] nor the winner who tried to weld a hand grenade onto a chain.[5] The stories assembled in this book show that common sense is really not so common.

There are people who think it's practical to solder an acetylene tank to a steel roof.[6] There are people who top off their car's brake fluid with dishwashing liquid.[7] We applaud the predictable demise of such daredevils with the Darwin Award, named after Charles Darwin, the father of evolution.

Darwin Awards show what happens to people who are bewilderingly unable to cope with obvious dangers in the modern world. The smoker who can't wait for the next stop and steps out of the bus to light up—at sixty miles an hour.[8] The father who shoots himself while proving that his son's instructor doesn't understand gun safety.[9] The camper with too much gear who stashes a propane tank in his car's engine compartment![10]

Darwin Award winners plan and carry out disastrous schemes that a child can tell are a really bad idea. They contrive to eliminate themselves from the gene pool in such an extraordinarily idiotic manner that their actions ensure the long-term survival of our species, which now contains fewer idiots. The single-minded purpose and self-sacrifice of each

[5] KILLS BUGS DEAD, page 132
[6] CHIMNEY-CLEANING GRENADE, page 188
[7] WELDING WARNING, page 204
[8] CLEAN BRAKE, page 57
[9] DYING FOR A CIGGIE, page 107
[10] GUN-SAFETY NONSENSE, page 246
[11] HAPPY CAMPER, page 58

winner, and the spectacular means by which he snuffs him-self, qualifies him for the dubious honor of winning a Darwin Award.

THE RULES

To win, nominees must significantly improve the gene pool by eliminating themselves from the human race in an astonish-ingly stupid way. Contenders are evaluated using the following five criteria:

Reproductive Dead End: The candidate must remove himself from the gene pool.

The Darwin Awards celebrate the self-removal of incom-petent genetic material from the human race. The potential winner must therefore render himself deceased, or at least in-capable of reproducing. If someone does manage to survive an incredibly stupid feat, then his genes ipso facto have some-thing to offer in the way of luck, agility, or stamina. He is there-fore not eligible for a Darwin Award, though sometimes the story is too entertaining to pass up and he earns an Honorable Mention.

The Darwin Awards community has engaged in inter-minable and ultimately inconclusive discussions about what it means to be removed from the gene pool. What if the winner has already reproduced; is it sufficient that she can make no further contributions? What if the nominee has an identical twin? Are women past childbearing age disqualified? What about cryogenics, which makes it possible for sperm and ova to outlive their donors? Cloning might eventually allow those who die from licking poisonous toads to reproduce post-humously, with disastrous effects on future generations!

It would take a team of researchers to ferret out the full reproductive implications of each nominee—a luxury Ms. Darwin lacks. Therefore, no attempt is made to determine the actual reproductive potential of the candidate. If you no longer have the physical wherewithal to breed with a mate on a desert isle, then you are eligible for a Darwin Award.

Excellence: The candidate must exhibit an astounding misapplication of judgment.

We are not talking about common stupidities such as for-getting soup on the stove, leaving the iron on, or jumping off the garage roof into a deep pile of leaves. The fatal act must be of such idiotic magnitude that we shake our heads and thank our lucky stars that our descendants won't have to deal with, or heaven forbid breed with, descendants of the buffoon that set that scheme in motion.

Baking bullets in an oven,[1] looking inside a rocket launcher,[2] clubbing chickens with the butt of a loaded gun,[3] jamming your head into a paper-towel dispenser,[4] and grabbing defibrillator paddles[5] while shouting, "Juice me up!" are are all worthy Darwinian activities.

[1] BAKED BULLET SURPRISE, page 241
[2] ROCKETING TO GLORY, page 195
[3] TESTOSTERONE, CHICKENS, AND GUNS, page 243
[4] HUMAN PAPER TOWEL, page 278
[5] JUICE ME UP!, page 280

Self-selection: The candidate must be the cause of his own demise.

The candidate's own gross ineptitude must be the cause of the incident that earns him the nomination. A driver hit by a falling tree is a victim of circumstance. If you chain the tree to your pickup and pull it over onto yourself,[6] you are a candidate for a Darwin Award.

Some think that a person who intentionally attempts to win a Darwin Award—and succeeds—is by definition a perfect candidate. However, I do not want to encourage risk-taking behavior, so anyone who purposely tries to join these illustrious ranks is automatically disqualified.

Maturity: The candidate must be capable of sound judgment.

People with physical or mental handicaps are more susceptible to doing themselves harm. Their deaths are not amusing, because their increased risk comes from an innate impediment, rather than poor decisions. Those who lack maturity are therefore not eligible for an award.

Children (typically below the age of sixteen) do not qualify, as their judgment has not fully developed. They do not possess sufficient maturity and experience to make life-or-death judgments, and the responsibility for their safety still resides with their guardians.

The maturity rule is not a foolproof way to duck a Darwin Award. For instance, if a person duct-tapes his wheelchair[7] to

[6] TREE VS. MAN, page 42
[7] WILD WHEELCHAIR RIDE, page 63

the back of a pickup truck—without securing himself to the wheelchair—he is eligible for a Darwin Award when he is tossed off while rounding a sharp corner. Or if a bar patron impairs his judgment by drinking copiously before accepting a bar bet, he is eligible for a Darwin Award when he can't remove the condom full of beer[8] from his esophagus.

Veracity: The event must be verified.

Reputable newspaper or other published articles, confirmed television reports, and responsible eyewitnesses are considered valid sources. Your brother's friend's boss, a chain email, or a doctored photograph are not.

THE CATEGORIES

This book contains three categories of stories.

- **Darwin Awards** nominees lost their reproductive capacity by killing or sterilizing themselves. This is the only category eligible to win a Darwin Award.
- **Honorable Mentions** are foolish misadventures that stop short of the ultimate sacrifice, but still illustrate the innovative spirit of Darwin Award candidates. We have changed names and obscured some details in these stories, to preserve a measure of anonymity for the participants.
- **Personal Accounts** were submitted by loyal readers blowing the whistle on stupidity, and are plausible but usually

[8] A MEDICAL FIRST AT OKTOBERFEST, page 169

unverified narratives. In some cases readers submitting Personal Accounts have been identified with their permission, but this does not necessarily mean that the sources are directly associated with their Personal Accounts.

Darwin Awards and Honorable Mentions are known or believed to be true. Look for the words *"Confirmed by Darwin"* under the title, which generally indicates that a story has been backed up by multiple submissions and by more than one reputable media source.

"Unconfirmed by Darwin" indicates fewer credible submissions and the unavailability of direct confirmation of media sources. In unconfirmed Darwin Awards, names have often been changed and details altered to protect the innocent (and, for that matter, the guilty).

PICKING THE WINNERS

Contenders are selected based on the five criteria of death, self-selection, excellence, maturity, and veracity. But there's more to the selection than one person making a dry comparison with the rules. The selection is a participatory event, a community celebration of the humor found in the inevitable results of foolish choices! Here's how the entire process works.

Submission

A Darwin Award begins its life as a submission to the website. The nominations come from around the world. Enthusiasts are encouraged to keep a sharp lookout for potential contenders in their neighborhoods and local newspapers. Amus-

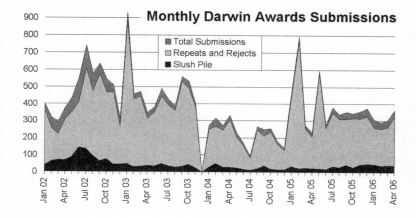

Monthly Darwin Awards Submissions

- Total Submissions
- Repeats and Rejects
- Slush Pile

ingly written stories are more likely to pass the triple hurdles of moderation, public vote, and Wendy's review.

Moderator Review

Each submission is reviewed by volunteer moderators who decide whether it's a potential Darwin Award, Honorable Mention, or Personal Account. Two to five moderators examine each story before it's moved to the public Slush Pile. Submissions that don't make the cut are usually repeats, bizarre or macabre stories, or illustrations of poetic justice, rather than examples of Darwinian self-selection.

As the graph illustrates, an average of five hundred stories are submitted per month, and approximately one in six is accepted into the Slush Pile. When a particularly sensational story appears in the news, it can be submitted hundreds of times. The spike in January 2003 was due to the shooting

death of a man who decided to beat his misbehaving dog with a loaded gun. The spike in July 2002 was caused by two men fighting over who would go to heaven and who to hell; a shotgun was used to solve the argument.

January 2005 brought the story of the handstand queen.[9] February 2006 featured a disappointed rugby fan who snipped off his own testicles with wire cutters. And in May 2005, two Star Wars acolytes constructed "light sabres" by filling fluorescent tubes with petrol. The chasm of zero submissions is from the Infamous Hacker Attack of Thanksgiving 2003.

Public Review

The stories, with moderator scores and comments appended, are transferred to the website, and the submitter is notified by email. The decision may be appealed; however, the moderators are fairly experienced, so decisions are only infrequently reversed. A submission will occasionally be removed for privacy reasons, or if it is the cause of many complaints.

**Readers rate the stories in the Slush Pile
on a scale from 0 to 10. Your vote counts!**

www.DarwinAwards.com/slush

[9] WHAT I CAN STILL DO, page 110

Wendy's Review

After at least a month of public review, I sort the Slush Pile based on popularity and begin reading through the submissions for that month. I refer to the moderator comments and decide whether each story is novel enough, and amusing enough, to write into a Darwin Award, Honorable Mention, or Personal Account. Approximately ten to fifteen stories per month are selected to enter the permanent archive.

The Final Cut

But that's not the end of the process! In fact, it's a new beginning, for stories in the archive enjoy a far greater audience than when they first appeared in the Slush Pile. Visitors read five million stories per month, and mistakes, corrections, and confirmations are frequently reported. The Darwin Awards are continually updated (or removed) based on new information, and this final review process continues for as long as the story remains on the website.

The accounts in this book have all been subject to this public scrutiny and are accurate to the best of my knowledge. But because the Darwin Awards are dynamic, they are not guaranteed to be entirely accurate, nor in their final form.

As you read the tales contained herein, keep in mind the lengthy submission process, as well as the care with which each gem was culled from dozens of competitors and honed to its current form.

HISTORY OF THE DARWIN AWARDS

The origin of the first Darwin Award is obscure.

I fancifully hypothesized that the collective processing power of connected computers that formed the early Internet gave rise to an electronic consciousness, and that the Darwin Awards were this artificial life-form's first successful attempt at humor. But recently, more information has come to light.

According to Google's Usenet archives, the first citation in August 1985 referred to the fellow who pulled a soda machine onto himself while trying to shake loose a free can. The second citation was five years later, when the Urban Legend of the JATO Rocket Car surfaced. The author of that Usenet posting, Paul Vixie, credited Charles Haynes. I didn't know how to contact Paul Vixie, or who he was. Along came Greg Lindahl, who opined, "Paul Vixie? Everybody knows who he is, he maintains BIND, which holds the Internet together." So Greg wrote Paul an email. Paul, a consummate pack rat, produced a 1991 email from Charles Haynes in which Charles said that he heard the term from Bob Ayers: "We normally sit around talking about Darwin Awards after a hard day's rock climbing. I wonder why . . ." At that point, the trail grew cold. Greg followed a few more leads, but was unable to track down earlier Darwin Awards.

My involvement with the Darwin Awards began in 1993. My cousin Ian emailed me one, and the tongue-in-cheek look at human evolution amused and tickled my scientific funny bone. I wanted more! But I could only find five, and tracing the Darwin Awards to their lair proved fruitless.

In 1993, I began writing new vignettes for my website as a hobby. I sent out newsletters, encouraged submissions, discussions, and voting. My hobby became a consuming passion, as I assumed the alter ego "Darwin" and debated philosophy with readers. These conversations led to the refinement of the concept of a Darwin Award.

I let the Darwin Awards grow under the guidance of the readers. I pruned stories when they told me my judgment was flawed; for instance, if the deceased was the victim of a bizarre accident rather than his own poor judgment. We argued fine points such as whether offspring or advanced age ruled out a candidate. And through the years, I protected my audience from submissions that would make a hardened criminal cringe! I said NO to pictures of gory accidents, sad tales of impoverished people, politically biased stories, racial stereotypes, and just plain mean submissions.

And I dealt with flames sympathetically. When community or family members wrote, I respectfully listened to their point of view. Our discussions sometimes led to that particular story being removed. Other times, the family realized that their tragedy could have the small solace of helping others avoid the same mistake, if they let it be used as a "safety lesson."

Part of the success of the Darwin Awards lies in the fact that we see a little of ourselves in every story. As one of the world's biggest klutzes, my final hour will likely find me clutching a Darwin Award. If so, I know my family and friends will laugh through their tears, and say, "That's just like Wendy. Oh, she was such an idiot!"

In 2000, my passion for this once-obscure Internet humor led to the publication of the first Darwin Awards book. And now *The Darwin Awards Movie* has been produced, starring Joseph Fiennes and Winona Ryder. But the heart and soul of the Darwin Awards is still on the Internet.

All the stories are available free on the website, updated with facts and comments from readers. The Slush Pile is brimming with new submissions. My goal is to maintain a network of people who love the Darwin Awards, and to keep this cultural icon true to its origins.

SURVIVAL OF THE FITTEST

Evolution is the process of a species changing over time to better suit its environment. The mechanism of evolution was referred to as "survival of the fittest" by Alfred Russell Wallace, the codiscoverer of evolution. He thought that the term "natural selection," coined by Charles Darwin, incorrectly implied a directed force behind the selection—i.e., an intelligent design. In a sense, what is most intelligent about the process of evolution is its utter simplicity: the ability to improve a species incrementally over thousands of generations, all through differences in individual rates of reproduction, aided by the raw material of random mutations.

Evolution gradually eliminates drivers who weave around on the freeway while yakking on a cellphone or typing on a laptop, or the more spectacularly foolish acts that earn Darwin Awards, like the men who tried to see who could hang the longest off a busy freeway overpass.[10]

There are many biological questions answered by evolution. For instance, humans apparently began wearing clothes seventy thousand years ago, according to the silent testimony of the lice that inhabit us. The human head louse lives on the scalp, while the body louse lives in clothing. The two lice genetically diverged when we began wearing fabric clothing, creating a

[10] FREEWAY DANGLER, page 157

Blanketing the Earth with squirrels

- Surface area of Earth: 197 million square miles
- Area covered by a squirrel: 0.2 square feet
- Number of squirrels needed to cover Earth: 25.5 quadrillion (25,500 trillion)

Squirrel math

- Pairs of squirrels have 2 litters of 3 pups every year, and they live for about 4 years, so a single pair could multiply to 25.5 quadrillion in just over 32 years.

The number is 19.4 quadrillion in 32 years, and 63.9 quadrillion in 33 years. Trust me. The complicated algorithm was generated by a real mathematician. (He assumed that squirrels float.)

(Unfortunately, squirrels are not drawn to scale.)

At this scale, where 1/4 inch = a trillion squirrels, this chart would go **530 feet** off the top of the page to represent 25.5 quadrillion squirrels. That's just under the height of the Washington Monument.

3 years:
20 squirrels

5 years:
210 squirrels

24 years:
1.4 trillion squirrels

YEARS   5   10   15   20   25   30

TRILLIONS OF SQUIRRELS

Chart by Nigel Holmes

new habitat. Researchers are now trying to date when humans lost their body hair, by analyzing the genes of pubic lice.

Yet despite the evidence, creationists continue to use squirrelly logic (squirrelly: cunningly unforthcoming or reticent) to claim that there is no such thing as evolution. So let's use our furry little friends, the squirrels, to illustrate the principles of natural selection.

In order for "survival of the fittest" to cause a species to evolve there are four requirements. 1) The species must show variation, and 2) that variation must be inheritable. 3) Not all members of the population survive to reproduce, but 4) the inherited characteristics of some members make them more likely to do so.

Wild adult squirrels can live about four years, and they have two litters of three pups every summer. Given these numbers, a single pair of squirrels could multiply to sixty-four quadrillion in thirty-three years if they all survived. That's more than enough squirrels to blanket the entire surface of the planet! Obviously, most squirrels do not reproduce so prolifically.

If you spend time watching squirrels, you will see that some are fatter than others, some hide better, and some are more aggressive about obtaining food. Because not all squirrels survive to reproduce, there is a selective pressure that favors inherited traits that play a role in survival. The parents of each new generation are the most successful squirrels from the past summer. Thus, successful traits become more prevalent over time, and less successful traits eventually disappear.

Like squirrels, not all humans survive to reproduce. Case in point is the human who dies clutching a Darwin Award. Although we regret his passing, we claim (tongue in cheek) that he has done the rest of us a favor, by sacrificing himself, thereby ensuring that our children don't have to breed with his children in the next generation.

ORIGIN OF THE NOVEL SPECIES *NOODLEOUS DOUBLEOUS*: EVIDENCE FOR INTELLIGENT DESIGN

Thomas D. Schneider, Ph.D.

Abstract

Penne rigate spontaneously inserts into *Rigatoni* (order *pasta*) under liquid to gas transition conditions of H_2O to create the previously unobserved species *Noodleous doubleous*. The estimated probability of this spontaneous generation event is too low to be explained by thermodynamics, and therefore apparently represents Intelligent Design.

Introduction

Intelligent Design advocates* claim that patterns observed in nature with a sufficiently low probability of occurence provide direct evidence for intelligent design, i.e., God. Here I report evidence for the spontaneous formation of a new life form in a prebiotic *pasta* soup.

Materials and Methods

Two point five L of pre-filtered, activated carbon–filtered, and reverse-osmosis purified H_2O was poured into a 24.0 cm (inner diameter) 4.7 L open metal nonstick-coated container to a final depth of 5 cm, and brought to 100 degrees C (liquid to gas

*Intelligent Design is Involved in the Origin of The Species (IDIOTS).

transition). No NaCl was added. Forty pieces each of *Penne rigate* and *Rigatoni* were dropped into the boiling H_2O. At five-minute intervals the mixture was stirred with a flat lignin paddle. At ~18 minutes the mixture was stirred a final time and then poured through a rigid plastic netting (square holes, sizes 3 mm x 4 mm and 4 mm x 4 mm) to capture the final products.

Figure 1: Sample of *pasta* captured from its native environment.

Results

Figure 1 shows a randomly collected sample from the native environment in which several *Penne rigate* are inserted into *Rigatoni*. The sample *pasta* are suspended on the flat lignin paddle. Three *Rigatoni* (60 percent) contain *Penne rigate* inserts. Note that a portion of the environment can be observed

Figure 2: Final population.

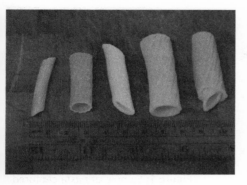

Figure 3: Components of *Noodleous doubleous*. From left to right: dry *P. rigate*; dry *Rigatoni*; *P. rigate* sampled at eighteen minutes; example *Rigatoni* sampled at eighteen minutes; example *P. rigate* inserted into *Rigatoni* to create *N. doubleous* sampled at eighteen minutes.

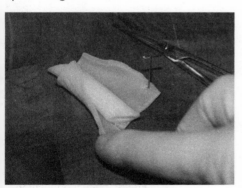

Figure 4: Dissection of *Noodleous doubleous*.

on the right side of the image as a white froth containing gas-enclosed sphericals. It is impossible to observe the *pasta* through this froth without disturbing the environment. There is some evidence for ordered patterning of the environment in which the *pasta* are oriented vertically, but this was destroyed by stirring. Note that the H_2O depth is substantially the same as the length of the two species of *pasta*.

Figure 2 shows the final population, in which 4 *N. doubleous* are visible. Conditions were no longer authentic *al dente* at the end of the experiment, and the violence of the trawling capture probably disturbed the neophytes. This could account for the reduced

number of observed *N. doubleous* compared to the rapid sampling shown in Figure 1.

Figure 5: *N. doubleous* observed in heat-source-detached environment. Note three bubble plumes emerging from the dorsal end of *Rigatoni* tubes.

As shown in Figure 3, boiled *P. rigate* (length ~5.0 cm, outer diameter 1.0 cm) can just barely fit inside boiled *Rigatoni* (length ~5.3 cm, inner diameter 1.3 cm) with a clearance of perhaps 0.15 cm. Under the turbulent thermal conditions, sliding one *pasta* tube into the other should be strongly disfavored.

To examine the internal organs, an *N. doubleous* was dissected (Figure 4). We note that the two subspecies fit together closely.

The tissue of *P. rigate* is notably lighter than that of *Rigatoni*. Also evident was the smooth interior wall of *Rigatoni*.

To confirm the results, the experiment was repeated. In an attempt to observe native conditions, the environment was gently removed from the heat source without stirring. Although this allowed cooling, it is likely that the configuration of the *pasta* is similar to its configuration in the native frothy environment. Figure 5 documents two related phenomena. First, *Rigatoni* are frequently oriented vertically while many *P. rigate*

Table 1: IDIOTS** calculation	
Rigatoni length (cm)	5.3
Rigatoni outer diameter (cm, from Figure 4)	1.7
Rigatoni cylinder surface (length × outer diameter × π), cm²	28.3
Rigatoni cylinder ends ((outer diameter/2)² × π × 2), cm²	4.5
Rigatoni total surface (side + ends), cm²	32.8
Inner diameter of *Rigatoni*, cm	1.3
The tip of *P. rigate* is pointy, with a diameter of 0.3 cm (Figure 3), reducing its effective size for slipping into *Rigatoni*. The target area the tip can enter: (2 × π × ((inner diameter—tip)/2)²), cm²	1.571
Probability of one insertion during a random encounter is the target area divided by the *Rigatoni* total surface	4.78×10^{-02}
Fraction of observed insertions (Figure 1)	0.6
Number of available *Rigatoni*	40
Estimated total number of insertions (40 × 0.6)	24
Probability of all these insertions by random encounter	2.05×10^{-32}

** This calculation was performed according to standard Intelligent Design (IDiotic) methods. It was performed using the calc program with an input file "idiotic.calc."

are frequently oriented horizontally or at forty-five degrees to the vertical. Second, bubble plumes emerge from the dorsal end of *Rigatoni* tubes.

A calculation was performed to determine the probability of the observed insertion events (Table 1).

Discussion

This paper reports an observation of spontanoodlus generation in which *Penne rigate* inserts within *Rigatoni* to create a new species dubbed *Noodleous doubleous*.

The Vertical Flow Hypothesis proposes that *Rigatoni* become vertically oriented in the convective flow of phase transitioning liquid H_2O, thereby increasing the heat dissipation rate.

This proposal is supported by the observation of bubble plumes on the dorsal side of *Rigatoni* (Figure 5). It is feasible that horizontally oriented *P. rigate* situated close to the bottom of the environment are drawn upward into the ventral side of *Rigatoni*. The *P. rigate* are not ejected from the *Rigatoni* because the dorsal end of the *Rigatoni* is close to the liquid surface and the process does not have sufficient energy to lift the *P. rigate* into the environmental froth. The *P. rigate* would therefore be caught inside the *Rigatoni*.

However, the probability of insertion events as proposed by the Vertical Flow Hypothesis is calculated to be extremely low (Table 1).

Conclusion

We conclude that the process was guided by some form of external intelligence. The experimenter did not perform this scalding task.

The high-temperature liquid was undergoing a rapid phase transition and liquid dihydrogen monoxide is extremely dangerous. Microscopic and macroscopic life forms were not observed in these extreme sterilizing conditions. Only an invisible macroscopic life form could have guided the rapid generation of the *Noodleous doubleous*.

We therefore conclude that this supernatural insertion process was done by the Hand of God.

A second viable hypothesis is that a divine Noodly Appendage of the Flying Spaghetti Monster was responsible for the effect. These results are therefore strong empirical support for Flying Spaghetti Monsterism.

Although it is considered unethical to destroy incipient lifeforms, thereby causing them to go extinct, the experimenter was hungry, so he ate them anyway.

References, complete experimental conditions, further reading:
www.DarwinAwards.com/book/noodles.html

Church of the Flying Spaghetti Monster:
www.DarwinAwards.html/book/spaghetti.html

Essay on Intelligent Design by Jason Stevens:
www.DarwinAwards.com/book/jason.html

CLEANING THE GENE POOL

The Darwin Awards that follow show that Nature is still improving on the human design. But they also illustrate the creativity that distinguishes us from less adaptable species. The same innovative spirit that causes the downfall of the Darwin Award winner is also responsible for the social and scientific advances that make the human race great.

CHAPTER 1

Vehicles

Motorcycles, trucks, trains, cars, snowmobiles, mopeds, a wheelchair, and one mountain bike—wheels spark a powerful urge to test mechanical limits. But to begin, an essay on human evolution. . . .

DISCUSSION: AIDS, BUBONIC PLAGUE, AND HUMAN EVOLUTION

Stephen Darksyde, Science Writer

Science teachers are often asked by skeptical students, "Why aren't people evolving now?" The answer, of course, is that evolution works on time scales far outside of normal human experience. To witness dramatic changes in form and function would require a lifespan encompassing thousands of generations. And evolution would operate much faster if humans lived in small, isolated populations, where a new gene can take hold and spread rapidly.

Evolution has been described as "goo to you" or "monkeys to men." But viewed as genetics, evolution is simply a change in the frequency of *alleles* (gene variations) in a population over time, as a result of natural selection. Humans number more than six billion. It would take many generations for a *single* beneficial gene to become fixed into that mass of humanity, much less enough genes to turn us into a new species. But we can observe a subtle change in gene frequencies happening right now as a consequence of natural selection. It involves AIDS, a gene for the chemokine receptor, and a mutant called Delta 32. And while some of those biogenetic terms may sound intimidating, with a dab of historical context and some basic biology, the story behind them is both comprehensible and fascinating!

Around the same time that HIV was found to be fatal despite aggressive treatment of AIDS complications, physicians noticed a mysterious twist. In a minority of patients the disease progressed at a markedly slower rate. These lucky few seemed resistant, though not immune. Stranger still, when accurate tests for HIV were developed, it was found that an even smaller group infected with HIV never developed any symptoms! The race was on to find out why HIV killed most—but not all. The answer would take researchers to a surprising place and time.

Six hundred years before the first AIDS patient stumbled into an emergency room, Europe was in the grip of another epidemic, the granddaddy of them all: the Black Death. Victims developed grotesque swellings in the armpits and groin, often so severe that their skin split open and body fluids seeped out by the pint. Blood congealed in the fingertips, feet, and lips, turning them black. Death followed quickly. Within weeks, once bustling city streets were littered with decaying bodies. What medical facilities existed broke down completely. Entire sections of London and Paris were deserted as terrified residents fled to the countryside, spreading the plague to every village as they went. It was *The Night of the Living Dead*—only it wasn't a movie. This was real.

The suspected primary culprit of the pandemic is *Yersinia pestis*, a bacterium carried by fleas living on rats which permeated the large, filthy cities of the era. *Y. pestis* infection does result in pronounced swelling of the lymph nodes, but it doesn't explain everything. The pattern of infection, the geographic distribution of specific symptoms, and modern research on

infectious disease all suggest there was more ravaging the people of Europe than a single disease.

The Black Death, also known as bubonic plague, affects the immune system. As with HIV victims, the plague patient is an easy target for opportunistic diseases: typhus, tuberculosis, smallpox, flu. What may have happened is that these diseases and others suddenly found their environment—human bodies—greatly weakened by the initial outbreak of bubonic plague initiated by *Y. pestis*. And like any organisms handed an opportunity to expand their domain, they radiated and evolved furiously. The result might have been a veritable stew of new superbugs able to overcome the resistance humans had developed to prior strains over thousands of generations.

Hundreds of millions died during the reign of the Black Death, and yet mysteriously, some survived infection, and others were immune. These lucky survivors were the beneficiaries of adaptations that had evolved in their genetic code.

So what does the Black Plague have to do with AIDS? Infectious pathogens gain entry to their victim's cells' by slipping through the cell membrane, a semipermeable outer wall. HIV bribes a molecular doorman called the "chemokine receptor" to get in. The blueprints for these receptors are, of course, found in our genes. In the lucky few patients who resist HIV, it was discovered that a gene involved in the construction of the chemokine receptor is defective. Constructing fewer receptors means fewer welcome mats for HIV.

This gene comes in a pair, one from each parent. If an individual has a single copy of the defective gene, there are fewer chemokine receptors on the cells, and HIV cannot infect them so easily. If both copies are defective, there are no receptors at all, and HIV is shut down cold by the body's defenses.

This life-saving genetic mutation, Delta 32, is found in higher frequencies in people with English, Scandinavian, and Germanic ancestry: the same population that took the brunt of the great plague. And as it turns out, the defective gene that we suspect conferred resistance to the Black Death all those centuries ago is the same one that gives resistance to HIV today!

In popular culture today, most people think of evolution as a fish growing legs, or monkeys turning into humans. In reality, only small changes occur from one generation to the next. But over time, those small changes add up. Eventually, the differences are large enough that an entirely new species splits off from an older parent population. Over really long periods, that process can transform a fish into an amphibian, or a tree-dwelling primate into a modern human.

Because of medical care, long generational spans, and a population in the billions, modern humans are evolving slowly, if at all. But given a big enough differential in mortality for selection to act on, we can pick up the pace as an evolving species. And more than five hundred years ago, in the midst of an epidemic that knocked off 25 percent of everyone alive, that's *precisely* what may have happened!

The stories in this chapter show that humans still have a long way to go in evolving to cope with the ubiquitous dangers of our transportation system. Vehicles can be hazardous to your longevity!

DARWIN AWARD: DARING FEET
Confirmed by Darwin
18 JULY 2004, TACOMA, WASHINGTON

Michael, 27, was spending a pleasant afternoon cruising on his motorcycle, and witnesses who saw him speeding down Meridian Avenue were not surprised when state troopers reported that he had lost control near the Kapowsin highway. You see, he was steering with his feet. Michael was killed instantly after being thrown from his motorcycle, which had veered to the right and hit a guardrail.

Reference: *Tacoma News Tribune*

DARWIN AWARD: RUTTING CONTEST

Unconfirmed by Darwin

OCTOBER 2004, TAIWAN

Most rutting contests involve two male mammals, like the Rocky Mountain bighorn sheep, *Ovis dallis*, which ram each other at high speed in order to impress a female sheep and win the right to procreate. These mammals tend to have unusually thick skulls and extra fluid surrounding the brain to prevent damage from the competition. Humans tend not to have such thick skulls and other natural adaptations, and therefore do not generally rut.

Of course, man, the tool user, can find artificial means to overcome natural limitations. One well-known example of this behavior is the medieval jousting contest, in which participants wear armor and ride horses toward each other at high speed.

The most recent observation of human rutting behavior occurred when two Taiwanese university students donned protective helmets and revved their motor scooters in an effort to impress a comely female of their species. The two were in the same class, but were not friends. Other classmates reported that both men fancied the same female student.

After indulging in a few drinks during the Mid-Autumn Festival, the two encountered each other, and words were spoken. The gauntlet was thrown down. In lieu of horses, the two would ride their motor scooters at each other at high speed, and the one who didn't turn away would win the exclusive right to pursue the female.

Obviously, both were very keen on her, because neither of them turned away. Their scooters collided head-on at fifty miles per hour. Both died instantly. The girl at the center of the rut refused to comment, other than to say that she "wasn't interested in either of them."

Reference: Major Taiwan media

Darwin Award: 4-1-0 Club

Confirmed by Darwin

14 October 2004, Missouri

When Peter and Jesse wanted to see what their new ride could do, like many young men, they got more than they bargained for. It was all fun and games until the vehicle stalled. In most cases this wouldn't be a serious problem—but Peter and Jesse stalled at forty-one thousand feet.

You see, they weren't pushing the old man's car to the limit. They were flying a fifty-passenger jet, a Bombardier CRJ200. Fortunately, there were no passengers aboard to share the fatal consequences.

Jesse, thirty-one, was the captain of Pinnacle Airlines Flight 3701, and Peter, twenty-three, was the copilot. They were transporting an empty plane from Little Rock, Arkansas, to Minneapolis, where it was needed for a morning flight. They decided to see what that baby could do. Their fun began while ascending, as they pulled 1.8 Gs in a maneuver that activated an automatic stall avoidance system.

Then they decided to "forty-one it," which meant taking the jet to forty-one thousand feet—eight miles—the maximum altitude the plane was designed to fly. The thrust of the engines pressed them into their seats with 2.3 times the force of gravity as they soared ever higher, laughing and cursing in a friendly manner, ignoring the overheating engines and the stick shaker that warned they were operating outside safe aerodynamic parameters.

At this point, air traffic control contacted the pilots to find

out what they were up to. A female controller's voice crackled over the radio: "3701, are you an RJ200?"

"That's affirmative."

"I've never seen you guys up at forty-one there."

The boys laughed. "Yeah, we're actually a, there's ah, we don't have any passengers on board, so we decided to have a little fun and come on up here."

Little did they know that their fun was doomed when they set the autopilot for the impressive climb. They had specified the *rate* of climb rather than the *speed* of the climb. The higher the plane soared, the slower it flew. The plane was in danger of stalling when it reached forty-one thousand feet as the autopilot vainly tried to maintain altitude by pointing the nose up.

"Dude, it's losing it," said one of the pilots.

"Yeah," said the other.

Our two flying aces could have saved themselves at that point. An automatic override began to pitch the nose down to gain speed and prevent a stall. Regrettably, Jesse and Peter chose to overrule the override. Oops. The plane stalled.

"We don't have any engines," said one.

"You gotta be kidding me," said the other.

Jesse and Peter still might have saved themselves. They were within gliding range of five suitable airports. Unfortunately, they did not reveal the full extent of their difficulties to the controller. They said that they had lost only one of the two engines. They glided for fourteen full minutes, losing altitude all the way. As they drifted closer and closer to the ground at high speed, still unable to get the engines restarted, they finally asked for assistance: "We need direct to any airport. We have a double engine failure."

Unfortunately, it was too late. "We're going to hit houses, dude," one of pilots said, as they desperately tried to reach an airport in Jefferson City. They missed the houses and the runway, crashing two and a half miles from the airport. Both men died in the crash.

"It's beyond belief that a professional air crew would act in that manner," said a former manager of Pinnacle's training program for the Bombardier CRJ200.

Reference: *New York Times*, NTSB, aero-news.com

DARWIN AWARD: AUTO BLOTTO

Unconfirmed by Darwin

7 SEPTEMBER 1990, SYDNEY, AUSTRALIA

Men seem to have an affinity for large trucks. What else can explain the actions of a thirty-four-year-old thief who decided to take possession of the engine of an old Bedford tip-truck?

The truck was parked outside a glass recycling company in Alexandria. It generally takes three men to lift an engine block of this size, but our enterprising pilferer decided that the best way to remove the engine was from below, rather than the conventional out-the-top-with-a-hoist technique.

He crawled under the cab and began to loosen the bolts.

Suddenly the engine block broke loose and landed on his face, killing him instantly. Police ascertained that he had at least one accomplice, judging by the pool of vomit found under a nearby bush.

An employee discovered his body early the next morning. The manager said that the truck was about to be scrapped. "If he had come and asked me for it, I would have given it to him."

Reference: *Australian Police Journal*, Vol. 53, No. 2, June 1999

Readers comment that an engine block can't drop without removal of the whole drive train and cutting out the motor mounts and bracing. Possibly it was the transmission or gearbox that fell on him, not the engine.

DARWIN AWARD: STEPPING OUT
Confirmed by Darwin
12 APRIL 2004, THE NETHERLANDS

Certain land animals have evolved over the millennia to use speed in the pursuit of prey or avoidance of predators. The cheetah (*Acinonyx jubatus*) can run as fast as 60 mph over the plains of Africa, and the pronghorn antelope (*Antilocapra americana*) can reach 55 mph over the plains of North America. Humans (*Homo sapiens*) are not among the animals built for speed. So things were bound to go wrong when a nineteen-year-old male, driving the A67 highway near Blerick, sought to impress his two passengers by putting his car on cruise control at 20 mph, getting out of the car, and running alongside it. He planned to jump back in and drive on, but the moment his feet hit the ground, he fell over and slammed headfirst into the asphalt. He died the next day.

Reference: Telegraaf, Dutch Teletext, *Guinness Book of World Records*

According to the <u>Guinness Book of World Records</u>, the fastest 100m dash time is less than ten seconds, resulting in an average speed of 23 mph from a dead stop.

Sprinting in the <u>Guinness Book of World Records</u>
www.DarwinAwards.com/book/guinness.html

Darwin Award: The Nuisance of Seat Belts

Confirmed by Darwin

5 January 2005, USA

In September of his senior year at the University of Nebraska, twenty-one-year-old Derek wrote an impassioned declaration of independence from seat belts for his college newspaper. Although "intrusive and ridiculous" seat-belt laws saved 6,100 lives a year, according to statistics from the U.S. Congress, Derek concluded with the statement, "If I want to be the jerk that flirts with death, I should be able to do that."

Derek "was a bright young boy, a 4.0" majoring in five subjects and planning to attend law school. But good grades don't always equate with common sense.

Derek was returning from a holiday in San Antonio, Texas. The driver of the Ford Explorer and his front-seat passenger both wore seat belts. Only Derek was willing to buck the system, sitting without a seat belt in the back seat because, in his own words, he belonged to the "die-hard group of non-wearers out there who simply do not wish to buckle up, no matter what the government does."

When the SUV hit a patch of ice, slid off U.S. 80, and rolled several times, Derek, in an involuntary display of his freedom, was thrown from the vehicle. He died at the scene. The other occupants of the SUV, slaves to the seat belt, survived with minor injuries.

Alcohol was not involved in the accident.

Reference: *Lincoln Journal Star*

DARWIN AWARD: TERMINAL CREATIVITY
Confirmed by Darwin
3 APRIL 2004, OREM, UTAH

Bobby, fifty-one, had trouble getting his truck to start. He couldn't be in two places at once, working under the hood and pressing the accelerator. Why not take a handy ice scraper and wedge one end against the accelerator and the other end against the seat? Then he could get under the hood and bypass the starter by connecting terminals on the starter solenoid.

Success!

Unfortunately he had forgotten to put the truck in neutral and it began accelerating toward his neighbor's motor home. Police concluded that Bobby jumped in front of the truck to prevent it from crashing into the motor home. He was partly successful. A neighbor found him pinned between the truck and the motor home, nearly dead. Paramedics rushed him to Timpanogos Regional Hospital, where the would-be mechanic died from terminal creativity.

Reference: *Salt Lake Tribune, Provo Daily Herald*

DARWIN AWARD: JACK UP

Unconfirmed by Darwin
9 APRIL 2003, NEW ZEALAND

Phil needed to make repairs to the underside of his car. But when he jacked it up, there wasn't enough room for him to work. So he removed the car's battery, placed the jack on top of it, and set to work again, this time with plenty of elbow room.

Unfortunately for Phil, car batteries are not designed to carry much weight. The battery collapsed and the jack toppled, trapping him beneath the car. Unable to breathe due to the weight on his chest, he quickly expired in a pool of battery acid.

This incident is illuminated by two additional facts: First, Phil's occupation was accident prevention officer at a large food-processing plant. And second, ten years previous, he had been working under a car when the jack collapsed, trapping him and breaking one of his legs.

Some people just don't learn—even from their own mistakes.

Reference: Personal account of his work mate;
Daily News, Taranaki, New Zealand

DARWIN AWARD: TREE VS. MAN
Confirmed by Darwin
21 DECEMBER 2004, GEORGIA

It looked at first like a bizarre traffic accident. Smoke rose from the charred remains of a large tree that had toppled onto a smoldering pickup truck. The body of a man, burned beyond recognition, was found inside the truck. Investigators were puzzled. How could the truck have collided with a tree *behind* a house? Why did the tree fall onto the truck instead of *away* from it? And what had started the fire?

As the pieces of the puzzle snapped into place, it became clear that the dead man was the victim of his own device. Reggie, forty-seven, had offered to remove a tree behind his girlfriend's house. He borrowed his father's pickup truck, apparently in the belief that he could yank out the bottom of the tree, which would then, cartoon-like, fall away from the truck. He tied the truck to the tree and floored the accelerator.

The uprooted tree, pulled in the direction of the force, toppled onto the truck, crushing the cab and trapping Reggie. The still-running engine eventually overheated, starting a grass fire that ignited the truck's gas tank, turning it into a fireball that spread to the tree.

Mercifully for Reggie, police determined that he was probably dead before the truck caught fire.

Reference: AP

• DARWIN AWARD: TUNNEL VISION

Confirmed by Darwin
19 MARCH 2004, VIRGINIA
RARE DOUBLE AWARD!
DARWIN AWARD & HONORABLE MENTION

Paul, forty-eight, was an electrician for the state department of transportation (DOT). He and Zachary were part of a fifteen-person crew assigned to replace the lights in the Hampton Roads Bridge-Tunnel. The crew would ride through the tunnel in a converted dump truck that had a ledge on the back used to hold tools during the procedure. DOT uses a different truck for each side of the tube, because the ceiling in the eastbound tube is three feet higher than the ceiling in the westbound tube. The taller truck therefore had a tight squeeze returning through the westbound tube. Paul and Zachary should have paid more attention to this fact.

The crew had finished working on the eastbound tube. On the return trip to the office for their lunch break, Paul and Zachary chose to violate safety and rules, and rode on the high platform, facing backward, rather than climbing into the cab. Paul and Zachary learned one major reason for the rules when the truck turned into the westbound tunnel . . .

Perhaps they had forgotten that this tunnel was three feet lower than the one they had just left. Perhaps their safety helmets made them feel invincible. They soon learned otherwise. When his head hit the entrance of the tunnel Paul was knocked off the truck to his death. Zachary was sitting lower than Paul and survived with minor injuries, earning himself an Honorable Mention.

Reference: *Daily Press*, AP

DARWIN AWARD: DOPE ON A ROPE

Confirmed by Darwin

16 FEBRUARY 2004, SIMI VALLEY, CALIFORNIA

"The family that plays together, stays together."

Alan, a forty-three-year-old electrician, was hanging out with his seventeen-year-old son and the son's girlfriend. They were feeling cooped up, so they hopped the back fence to play by the railroad tracks that ran behind it.

> **"Dope on a Rope"** is also the search-and-rescue nickname for the practice of dangling a rescuer under a helicopter on a fixed rope, as opposed to a powered hoist, to assist a victim.

Alan thought it would be a blast to watch a shopping cart being dragged by a train. He tied one end of a twenty-foot rope to the shopping cart and the other to a full water bottle, which he planned to use as a weight.

When an eighty-six-car Union Pacific freight train rumbled through at fifteen miles per hour, Alan stood behind the cart and hurled the bottle at the train. The bottle broke! So he quickly tied another bottle to the rope. *Standing in front of the cart*, he lobbed the bottle under the train, and gleefully noted that his plan had worked this time—until the shopping cart whipped into him and dragged him for more than a mile along the tracks, reportedly pulling up two spikes in the process.

Alan was dead before the engineer could stop the train. A spokesman for the Federal Railroad Administration said that this was "an extremely unusual occurrence." Alan's son told reporters, "He was just the funniest guy."

After the incident, Simi Valley Police Sergeant Joe May warned pedestrians not to loiter near train tracks.

Reference: *Los Angeles Herald-Tribune, Ventura County Star*

DARWIN AWARD: DEATH VALLEY DAZE

Confirmed by Darwin

27 JULY 2005, CALIFORNIA

Robert, thirty-five, was eager to hang out with the nudists at the Palm Springs campground, in a part of Death Valley where temperatures reached 136 degrees Fahrenheit. The track was rough but passable until he was lured into the Saline Mud Flats by the deceptively dry appearance of its cracked surface, which radiated heat in the baking sun. Within a few feet, the wheels of his VW Microbus sunk deep into the muck hiding just beneath the crust.

Robert was miles from nowhere, surrounded by the bleached skulls of other animals that had become trapped in the mire. But he had plenty of provisions, so he waited for help to find him on the remote dirt track. After six days, he finally abandoned the microbus and began walking to a less deserted location where someone was more likely to pass.

Luck was with him! As he was shaking the last drop of water from his bottle, help arrived in the form of fourteen-year-old British lads from the League of Venturers, who were training in search-and-rescue techniques. "He was crying and completely hysterical. I don't think he expected to last the day," said the unit leader. They gave him a lift to the nearest ranger station, eighty miles away, where he kissed the ground in gratitude.

Robert had cheated death once, but that didn't stop him from tempting fate again.

In nearby Bishop, he found someone to tow the microbus out of the mud flats. Alas, it had two flat tires and other mechanical problems, so he returned to Bishop for automotive supplies. He snagged another ride into Death Valley, this time with a couple who took an unfamiliar route from the north, and dropped him off at a washout in the road about fifteen miles from the Palm Springs campground.

His plan was to locate the campground and enlist help fixing his vehicle. He stashed his supplies and began walking. His body was found three days later, without a map, a GPS, or even water. Authorities estimated that he had walked along the road for ten miles before heading into the open desert, seeking water.

Reference: *Southampton Echo*, UK; *Daily Record*, Glasgow, UK; www.death-valley.us; *Daily Mirror*; KCBS

DARWIN AWARD: TREE HARD, HEAD EMPTY

Confirmed by Darwin

17 FEBRUARY 2003, NEW YORK

A twenty-five-year-old man, long accustomed to annoying neighbors by snowmobiling at high speeds through sleeping streets, finally received his comeuppance—and in the process, a Darwinian nomination—when he drove headfirst into a tree.

It is not only his reckless speeding through a nighttime residential area that makes him eligible; nor is it merely because he was driving an unregistered, uninsured snowmobile without a helmet while drunk. Although these spectacularly stupid ideas were ultimately responsible for his demise, there is yet another relevant aspect to report.

Brian was a fireman, a member of the same company dispatched to peel him off the tree, the same organization that preaches snowmobile safety, responds to other gruesome snowmobile accidents, and the very same company that posts an illuminated "helmet safety" notice seven hundred feet from his own home.

Clearly, while others have been as foolish as Brian in their choice of recreational activities, few have been so uniquely aware of the possible concussions and repercussions prior to making that choice!

Reference: Personal account, AP, buffalonews.com, cable6tv.com

READER COMMENTS:

"I don't think a helmet would have helped the last smart cell in his brain escape this one."

"The only way this could have been better is if he had contrived to hit the same pole that the 'helmet safety' sign was posted on. . . ."

Darwin Award: Heck on Wheels

Confirmed by Darwin

17 April 2005, Syracuse, Indiana

Late one night, twenty-six-year-old Joseph was blazing down a road in the Chain O'Lakes district on his Yamaha moped. When he saw flashing lights in his rear-view mirror, well . . . with the wind whistling in his ears, he apparently concluded that his moped could outrun a police cruiser. This hard-boiled Heck's Angel revved his engine and roared off.

The speedometer needle flashed past ten, twenty, and then thirty miles per hour, and within a minute, it was in the red zone at a blinding forty. But no matter how fast Joseph went, he was unable to shake the pursuing police officer from his tail! If only he had a spare JATO!

The two-stroke engine was buzzing like a hummingbird from the strain of the chase. Perhaps he was thinking, "You'll never take me alive, copper!" as he sped through the intersection. Whatever his last thoughts may have been, Joseph lost control of his would-be road rocket, crashed into a tree, and died instantly.

Reference: *Warsaw Times-Union*, wlzq.com, wndu.com

DARWIN AWARD: SELF-DEMOLITION DERBY
Confirmed by Darwin
SEPTEMBER 2003, MINNESOTA

The purpose of a demolition derby is to smash into other cars. Crash, repair, repeat. As a result, in competition, derby cars become more fragile than the average car. So you would think that Scot, a derby car owner, would take this fact into account when he crawled under his car for repairs. Why take the time to put a car up on blocks? It would be faster and easier to use a handy Bobcat-type skid loader and just lift the car up from its bumper.

When the car was raised, Scot slid beneath. Then the bumper broke off. Help was immediately summoned, but it was too late. Scot had lost his final demolition derby.

Reference: *Detroit Lakes Tribune*

DARWIN AWARD: ASPHALT TATTOO

Confirmed by Darwin

1 SEPTEMBER 2003, COLORADO

Ever since middle school, friends say, Tyler, 20, wanted to do something different, something unique, something nobody else would ever try: jump from a moving car. "He thought he could jump, roll, and stand," said a friend, "like you see in the movies." Tyler came away from an early car-jump experiment alive, with an asphalt tattoo to commemorate the feat.

On Labor Day, he was planning another dramatic stunt, riding in the back seat of a Subaru Legacy. Although his friends tried to talk him out of it, the Subaru was cruising at forty miles per hour when Tyler decided that he could, he should, he would jump from the car.

His father explained, "I think this was the last big thing he wanted to do as an immature kid, before accepting he had to grow up." But plans to mature were cut short by his instant death, as he hit the road one last time. Tyler's final jump is commemorated with another asphalt tattoo, this one shaped like a Darwin Award.

Reference: *Rocky Mountain News*

HONORABLE MENTION: OVERHEATED ENGINE

Confirmed by Darwin

7 JANUARY 2004, CROATIA

"Maybe I used too much paper."

Eastern Europe is known for its harsh winters, and Dusan, fifty-two, had weathered his fair share of them in his town. But when temperatures dropped low enough to play havoc with outdoor machinery, Dusan was exasperated to find that his Opel Kadett had fallen victim to the cold, repeatedly refusing to start.

The engine must be frozen, he decided. He remembered times he himself had been freezing in those icy Croatian winters. There was nothing better than warming up before a toasty roaring fire. Yes! That was clearly the solution to his problem. A roaring fire would warm up the Opel's engine.

Dusan fetched some old newspapers, stuffed them under the engine, and lit them. While waiting for the engine to warm up, he wandered off—a fortunate occurence, because his beloved car exploded in a fireball. The heartbroken man told reporters, "I couldn't start the engine and realized it was frozen. Now my lovely car is destroyed."

Luckily, Dusan has identified what went wrong.

"Maybe I used too much paper," he said.

Reference: ananova.com

Before fuel preheaters were installed in diesel engines, it was common for fires to be lit under frozen engines to thaw out the fuel. Because diesel is a safer fuel, this is less problematic than lighting a fire in a petrol (gasoline) engine.

When a story is about a person who is still with us, the name is changed. In this case, I selected a Croatian name meaning, "God is my judge."

HONORABLE MENTION: CLEAN BRAKE

Confirmed by Darwin

5 NOVEMBER 2004, NEW ZEALAND

Sometimes it pays to use a cheaper substitute, thought Shane, nineteen, as he replaced lost brake fluid with dishwashing liquid. He took the car out for a test drive and discovered that sometimes you get what you pay for.

He applied his foot to the brake pedal as the car began to slide around a slight bend, but for some reason, the brakes didn't respond. The car spun completely around, clipped the curb, and slammed into a power pole.

His trouble was just beginning, though, because Shane had also saved money by not registering the car. There was really no point in registering the car, he thought, because his license had already been suspended. Shane was sentenced to two hundred twenty hours of community service for driving with a suspended license, dangerous driving, and stealing two orange traffic safety cones.

For what it's worth, his license was suspended for another year.

Reference: *New Zealand Herald*

HONORABLE MENTION: HAPPY CAMPER
Unconfirmed by Darwin
CAMPING SEASON 2003, MELBOURNE, AUSTRALIA

Emergency services was called to attend to a motor-vehicle fire on the Monash Freeway, a beltway around Melbourne. On arrival they found an agitated young man watching his car go up in smoke.

After extinguishing the fire, they inspected the small four-cylinder vehicle, which was tightly packed with camping gear. Upon raising the hood, they discovered the cause of the fire: smoldering camping gear that had been stashed in the engine bay, including a bottle of gas used for a portable barbecue!

The driver explained that he was taking an extended camping trip and had run out of room in the passenger compartment, so he decided to use all that "wasted space" in the engine bay.

Our Aussie correspondent says, "I reckon that the only waste of space was between this bloke's ears. If the fireys hadn't arrived when they did, we would have had the first Ford in orbit."

Reference: Channel 9 News

HONORABLE MENTION: PICTURE-PERFECT COP

Confirmed by Darwin

7 AUGUST 2003, WYOMING

Like a true country child, Tom was born, born to be wild . . . even though he had grown up to be a county sheriff. The wild one had taken to the road in the company of another lawman and his brother, riding his hog without a helmet to the big motorcycle rally in South Dakota.

No road trip would be complete without a commemorative photograph. With the wind streaming through his hair at sixty-five miles per hour, Tom decided the conditions were right. He took his camera and turned around to take a picture of the bike behind him. This of course required the bold Harley rider to take his hands off the handlebars.

As a state trooper described it later, the motorcycle drifted to the right and headed for a telephone pole. Tom lost control trying to wrestle the bike back onto the highway and went sailing through the air, probably wishing he had worn his helmet after all. When he landed, he broke his eye socket, four ribs, and a shoulder bone, and suffered other head injuries and road rash. There's no word on whether he got the photograph or not.

Tom had been following a beloved motto: "No Helmets 4 Harleys." Although he miraculously survived, he nearly proved another adage: "There are old riders, and bold riders, but no old bold riders!"

Reference: Associated Press, *Casper Star-Tribune*

HONORABLE MENTION: NEW HOG

Confirmed by Darwin

1 OCTOBER 2002, MICHIGAN

Luke was pushing sixty when youthful memories of *Easy Rider* brought him to the local Harley-Davidson dealership. "It was a mid-age crisis," he told a reporter. "I'd see dudes with women and thought a motorcycle would put me in like Flynn."

When the dealer delivered the gleaming new hog to Luke's front door, his eyes lit up like a boy receiving a Red Ryder two-hundred-shot carbine air rifle with a compass in the stock—and no grownups around to warn him that his new toy could put an eye out!

Luke started the engine and felt its pulsing, guttural power. It had been thirty years since he had been in the saddle of a babe-magnet like this. He revved the engine and listened to it purr. He kicked it into gear and roared off down the road. Born to be wild!

Ten seconds and a tenth of a mile later, Luke slammed into a neighbor's utility trailer at forty miles per hour as he tried to re-member how the throttle worked. The cops who investigated told him it was a miracle he was alive. He survived with just a few broken ribs. "Oh my God," he said, "I hurt in places I didn't know could hurt."

Insurance covered repairs to the bike and the trailer. Luke sold the restored dream machine for $800 less than he paid, but every few weeks, he continues to receive mailings from his com-plimentary membership in the Harley Owners Group. Some dreams die hard.

Reference: AP

Personal Account: Blast from the Past
Mid-1950s, USA

My father and uncle were reminiscing about their youth, and they shared a rather Darwinian story. In their twenties, they succeeded in assembling one great car out of three junkers. After they accomplished this, they had enough parts left over to make a second working car—but only barely. This car was missing most of its floorboards, so they could see the ground flash past while driving. They called this a feature rather than a flaw, and decided to have fun with it.

In the fifties, high-powered explosives were still easy to acquire. So, with quarter sticks of dynamite readily available, my future father and his brother drove around throwing dynamite sticks through the gaps in the floorboards, basically scaring the daylights out of people in cars behind them. THIS WAS FUN! They even shortened the fuses to make sure that the sticks would "safely" explode before the car behind them drove over them.

When I heard this story, my first response was, "Weren't you concerned about the gas tank below you?" To my amazement, they both looked rather surprised, exchanged glances, and said, "We never thought of that!"

My grandfather just laughed and walked out of the room.

Reference: Eric Vane, Personal Account

PERSONAL ACCOUNT: BRAKE CARE
SUMMER 2001, USA

"The squeaky wheel gets the grease."

I am a keen mountain biker, and was the proud owner of a fairly expensive mountain bike. My bike was fitted with "V" brakes, which are extremely effective though prone to squealing.

My dear brother decided to have a ride on my bike one day while I was out. He noticed the squealing as he cycled down the hill we live on, toward the invariably busy crossroads at the bottom. Being a helpful sort, he headed back home and proceeded to pour a generous amount of 3-IN-ONE oil onto the brakes, before once more setting off down the hill.

The oil worked! The only reported squealing came from my brother, as he slammed into the side of a moving VW Beetle. To this day he sports an impressive scar running from his eye socket to just past his ear.

And yes, the bike was totaled.

Reference: Personal Account

PERSONAL ACCOUNT: WILD WHEELCHAIR RIDE
4 JULY 1995, SOMEWHERE IN THE USA

During my second year of residency in orthopedic surgery, a thirty-five-year-old roofer was admitted to the hospital after falling from a roof. His boss had told him to tie himself off to prevent a fall, but he was an experienced roofer and knew that wouldn't happen. Nevertheless, he fell off the roof, fracturing his pelvis, his right femur, and his left tibia. An avoidable accident, but certainly not worthy of a Darwin Award. The patient underwent surgery, and was discharged from the hospital after an uneventful three-day postoperative course.

So far, so good.

The patient returned by Care Flight nine hours later, looking worse than he had the first time. He had torn the external fixator from one side of his pelvis, fractured his femur below the rod that had been used to fix it the first time, and fractured his tibia above the rod used to fix that, as well. And he hadn't been anywhere near a roof.

It turned out that he and his brother-in-law had decided to go barhopping to celebrate his recovery. Since he was stuck in a wheelchair, they figured the best way to get him from bar to bar was to *duct tape his wheelchair* to the bed of the pickup truck. The plan worked perfectly all evening, as they got more and more soused. Now, if only they had duct taped the roofer to his wheelchair. . . .

They were on their way home when his brother-in-law took a corner too fast. The roofer shot out of his wheelchair and landed on the street.

The patient was repaired, and he recovered fully, much to the annoyance of natural selection. I don't know if he ties himself off when roofing these days, but he hasn't been back to my hospital. I'm not sure how long he'll remain in the gene pool, though, and he certainly deserves an Honorable Mention.

Reference: Personal Account

CHAPTER 2

Water

Water covers 70 percent of the Earth's surface, so it's little wonder that this is the medium in which many Darwin demises occur. We herein encounter the dangers of "snowmoboating," the tide, frozen rivers, raging rivers, two waterfalls, one bungee cord, and even the kitchen sink! But first, an essay on the Aquatic Ape hypothesis.

DISCUSSION:
AQUATIC APES ARE PEOPLE, TOO!

Stephen Darksyde, Science Writer

Not everyone is comfortable with the idea that humans are animals, or that we're apes. But the fact is, the cells that make up our bodies have nuclei and organelles such as mitochondria, we're capable of locomotion, and unlike plants we consume other organisms to survive. That's all it takes for an organism to be classified as an animal. And we're mammals, primates to be exact, with large brains and no external tails. That puts us in the class of hominids along with our closest cousins: the gorilla, chimpanzee, orangutan, and gibbon.

But humans do possess a number of unique attributes in our form and structure, the most obvious being that we are obligatory bipeds: We walk on two legs, and we don't have much choice about it. We're not the only large vertebrates to walk on two legs—dinosaurs, birds, and kangaroos are bipedal, but they're like teeter-totters, with their upper and lower bodies balanced over the fulcrum of their hips. Humans are like pogo sticks, with our heads balanced precariously atop a double-curved spine. This anatomy is unique in all the animal kingdom.

Our form of bipedalism comes with many drawbacks that

four-legged animals don't suffer from. Fallen arches, shin splints, hernias, and back problems are all caused by walking upright. Given the high price we pay for walking on two legs, it's tough to imagine what original, critical advantage was gained by our proto-bipedal ancestors, whose bodies were even less adapted to the rigors of bipedal locomotion.

Why we became bipedal is mystery enough, yet other oddities are even harder to explain!

Our unique human qualities also include being bald and chubby. We are nearly hairless, and to the detriment of our self-esteem, we carry a high body-fat content compared to most mammals. Much of the fat is stored just under our skin. Also unusual is that humans can control breathing beyond the capabilities of most mammals.

Enter Elaine Morgan, a feisty Welsh feminist and writer. In the early 1970s, Morgan began to develop and promote a controversial hypothesis seeking to unite a number of human oddities within a single explanatory framework. Her hypothesis is that human ancestors lived in close proximity to water for extended periods, and spent so much time beach-combing, wading, and diving for foodstuffs that they evolved to suit their environment. We're not merely apes, we're Aquatic Apes!

The Aquatic Ape Hypothesis is astonishing, but Morgan makes some good points. For starters, take bipedalism: If a chimp tried to maintain an erect posture, the physiological consequences would not bode well for the animal. Over time it would incur problems keeping its blood pressure up, and suffer skeletal damage as it repeatedly moved from an upright to a reclined position. But if a chimp or a gorilla were wading on two legs and supported by water, those problems would be

greatly reduced or eliminated. And there is an immediate survival benefit for a bipedal ape wading in three or four feet of water: The animal would have its head above the surface and be able to breathe! Given an immediate benefit, a new food supply to exploit, and the advantages of walking on two legs in water, natural selection would have a platform from which to work—and perhaps eventually craft apes that were obligatory bipeds.

The Aquatic Ape hypothesis explains our high body-fat content as more than energy storage: It represents critical insulation. Body hair prevents heat loss only when an animal is dry; however, a wet, furry mammal loses heat almost as fast as one with no hair. Among aquatic mammals—whales, walruses, and seals—hair is sparse, just as it is on our bodies. Most large mammals store subcutaneous fat for one of two purposes: seasonally for hibernation, or year-round because they're partially or fully aquatic.

Is the Aquatic Ape hypothesis valid? Any useful scientific hypothesis must make predictions that can be tested. If these predictions are validated through observation and experiment, then the hypothesis gradually becomes a scientific theory. The more data the theory unifies under a single coherent explanation, and the more successful its predictions, the stronger it becomes. If the evidence comes from independent sources that all interlock with the theory in a consistent manner, and this consistency keeps up as more and more information is discovered, then that theory will become part of the scientific consensus and you really have a winner.

Charles Darwin's original idea is an example of a hypothesis that became a theory. The evidence for common descent, one of the key predictions of the theory of natural selection, includes mountains of empirical data from the fossil record, molecular biology, and physiology. Common descent is so solidly supported by so many independent lines of evidence that it's considered an inferred fact by almost all scientists today.

To explain a few existing anatomical structures and physiological processes, the Aquatic Ape Theory is satisfactory. But we have little other evidence to support it.

In particular, the fossil record does not advance the Aquatic Ape conjecture. We have only a few fossil scraps of human ancestors from the time before bipedalism was well developed three million years ago, represented by the archetype *A. afarensis,* a.k.a. Lucy. And that's the critical period when an aquatic ancestral phase would have had to exist for it to explain the origin of bipedal locomotion. Even if we had a complete skeleton from the exact time and place required, how would we distinguish a partly aquatic hominid from a close relative that was not aquatic at all? It would be tough to peg a sea otter, a beaver, or a polar bear as partially aquatic from fossils, if we'd never seen such an animal in the flesh.

Some scientists think that the case Morgan makes has been overstated. Maybe there is a bit of elitism going on with a few of her critics; Elaine Morgan is not a paleontologist or an anthropologist by training. But some of the critics also put forth alternative explanations for the anatomical congruencies between humans and aquatic mammals. For example, people do store more fat than most of our land-dwelling mammalian relatives, but maybe that's because it's an effective reservoir of fluids, energy, and critical trace nutrients, all of which would be useful for a creature that moved from the steamy jungle to the arid plains.

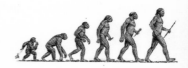

For now, the Aquatic Ape scenario remains an intriguing hypothesis and not much else. But science moves in mysterious ways. One can never predict what will be found next.

Now that we've investigated the possibility that humans evolved to live in a liquid habitat, let's dive into stories featuring water, where one soon sees that our evolutionary adaptations are not yet complete.

DARWIN AWARD: SNOWMOBOATER

Confirmed by Darwin

8 JULY 2001, MONTANA

From the time we climbed down from the trees to light a fire, we have been developing new and creative ways to make our lives easier. Centuries ago, the hardy Arctic people found that sliding on boards in deep snow was easier than walking, and when motors came along, an obvious improvement was to hook the two ideas together, making the snowmobile.

Even today, intrepid experimenters are finding new uses for the snowmobile. Although five-hundred-pound snowmobiles are not designed to float, and in fact do not float, people have discovered that they can hydroplane across the surface of the water. It's called "water skipping" or "snowmoboating."

Gary, forty-nine, did not know how to swim. Yet because he lived in Montana, where a man's gotta do what a man's gotta do, he found a way to enjoy water sports. Yes, water skipping had a new convert.

Demonstrating his manliness by not wearing no stinkin' life jacket, Gary climbed onto his snowmobile, gunned the motor, and skittered across the surface of the reservoir like a waterbug on speed. He zoomed onto the far bank, two hundred yards away. Great delight was expressed by all.

He turned the snowmobile around, gunned the motor like that other great Montana daredevil, Evel Knievel, and roared onto the water for the return trip. He had barely made it fifty feet when the snowmobile lost momentum. His buddies watched in horror as the snowmobile plunged to the bottom of the reservoir, carrying a white-knuckled Gary down with it.

Montana had seen its first drowning victim from water skipping.

Reference: *Peninsula Clarion*

Snowmoboating falls into a legal gray area. Unlike water-skiers and Jet Ski pilots, snowmobilers are not required to wear life jackets. And laws prohibiting driving motor vehicles into bodies of water don't apply to snowmobiles. After all, who would? Apparently enough people that a world championship water-skipping event is held every summer in Grantsburg, Wisconsin. The only state to ban the activity, after discovering the sport's potential for creating new Darwin Award candidates, is Nebraska.

DARWIN AWARD: SECOND TIME'S THE CHARM

Unconfirmed by Darwin
16 MARCH 2003, MICHIGAN

Ignoring Coast Guard warnings, David ventured onto the icy surface of Saginaw Bay with his pickup truck one chilly morning. Predictably, the vehicle broke through the ice, but the forty-one-year-old managed to avert tragedy and escape from the sinking truck. He reached the shore wet and cold, but alive.

Despite his traumatic experience, and despite a day of sunshine and warm temperatures in the sixties, David returned to Saginaw Bay late the following night. This time he was driving an all-terrain vehicle, and accompanied by a friend. Surprise! The ATV also plunged through the ice.

His companion survived, but David had used up his luck. His body was recovered by the Coast Guard southwest of the Channel Islands. An autopsy was scheduled to determine whether anything besides a desire to win a Darwin Award was a factor in his demise.

Reference: *Flint Journal*

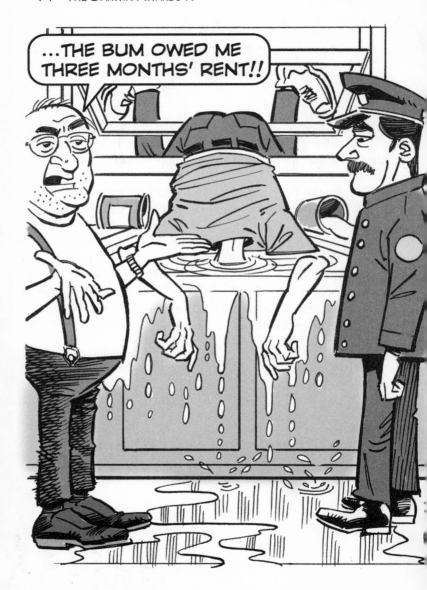

Darwin Award:
Man Drowns in Kitchen Sink

Confirmed by Darwin

26 May 2004, Austria

The manager of an apartment house was surprised to find the legs of a corpse sticking out of a tenant's window. Police entered the apartment and found the deceased man's head soaking in a sink full of hot water.

Apparently, the out-of-work Austrian had returned home after a night of drinking and drugs. He decided to slip in through the kitchen window. The window was fixed at the base and tilted out, giving him just enough room to squeeze his head through as far as the sink before he got stuck. While flailing around trying to escape, he turned on the hot water tap.

Police were not sure why he had not turned off the water, pulled the plug, or—perhaps most important—entered through the front door, since they found the keys in his pants pocket.

Reference: *Kurier* (Austria)

DARWIN AWARD: TIDE WAITS FOR NO MAN
Confirmed by Darwin
23 MAY 2005, CRYSTAL BEACH, TEXAS

After surf-fishing on Crystal Beach, John was fatigued but un-willing to call it a night. The full moon threatened to disturb his nap, so John curled up for forty winks in the darkest place available: underneath his truck, which was parked on the beach.

The next morning, a pickup truck was reported abandoned in the surf off Crystal Beach. A tow truck driver was called in, and had barely moved the pickup a foot, when he found the body of a thirty-seven-year-old man embedded in the sand beneath it.

It turned out that the truck was not abandoned, after all. As John slept, time passed and the tide rolled back in. The wet sand shifted beneath the truck's weight, and John was trapped beneath it, unable to escape. The beach became his final resting place.

Reference: *Houston Chronicle*, KLTV, KBTV

DARWIN AWARD: COLD CALL

Confirmed by Darwin

20 JANUARY 2004, VENTNOR, NEW JERSEY

"Proof that using a cell phone causes brain damage?"

A high school student accidentally dropped his cell phone from the Dorset Avenue Bridge. Fortunately, the river had frozen over, so the phone landed on the ice, apparently intact. To a dedicated user, losing one's phone is like losing an appendage. And what loyal friend would not try to retrieve your arm or leg if it had somehow fallen off a bridge and landed on thin ice? The survival of our species depends on mutual support.

Two days later, Bruce, seventeen, volunteered to fetch the phone. He figured that the ice, just an inch thick in places, was strong enough to hold him for the rescue mission. Another friend urged Bruce to give up and go back to shore. "I can do it," Bruce insisted.

A bridge attendant also warned him to stay off the ice, but as his mother explained, "It's just something Bruce would have done." The attendant rushed to his post to call the police. He was on the phone when a bystander told him that someone had fallen in. An officer arrived at the scene moments later to find Bruce partially submerged in the thirty-five-degree water. The officer dashed to his car for a rescue buoy, but when he returned, Bruce had already gone under. His body was recovered the next morning.

Bruce did not die in vain. The cell phone was recovered, as well.

10 FEBRUARY 2004, NEW YORK

Exactly three weeks later, eighteen-year-old Lina, of Queens, jumped onto the subway tracks to retrieve her new cell phone just as the V train was rounding the corner into the Grand Avenue station. She apparently expected to hop right back up onto the platform, five feet above the tracks, but after two attempts, she was still stuck. As the lights of the oncoming train shone in the tunnel, two men tried to pull her up, but she was knocked out of their hands as the train rushed into the station, emergency brakes squealing. She died along with her cell phone.

Reference: *Philadelphia Inquirer, New York Post, New York Daily News*

DARWIN AWARD: BOTTOM OF THE BARREL

Confirmed by Darwin
11 JULY 1920, NIAGARA FALLS,
BETWEEN ONTARIO AND NEW YORK

To support his wife and eleven children, Charles Stephens, the fifty-eight-year-old "Demon Barber of Bristol," needed more money than he could make giving shaves and haircuts. Even his sideline as a daredevil, performing high dives and parachute jumps in England, barely helped cover the bills. He needed something big, something to make his reputation. There was nothing bigger and more daredevilish than going over Niagara Falls in a barrel. Only two people had ever done it and lived.

It didn't matter that one, Annie Taylor, was living in abject poverty or that the other, Bobby Leach, was trying to talk him out of using his heavy Russian oak barrel without first sending it on a test run. Leach's friend, William "Red" Hill, a daredevil whose sideline was rescuing people from Niagara's treacherous waters, also tried to dissuade Charles.

But Charles believed that if he strapped his arms to the side of the barrel and his feet to a large anvil as ballast, he would pop up out of the foam at the bottom of the cataract, safe and right-side up. He knew what he was doing, by gum, and he was going to do it.

He launched his ungainly craft early one morning, and floated through the rapids toward Horseshoe Falls on the Canadian side. Forty-five minutes after launch, the heavy barrel flew over the edge of the falls. So far, so good . . . but when Charles hit the water below, the anvil plunged through the bottom of

the barrel, carrying most of Charles to the bottom with it. The barrel became stuck behind the falls. It wasn't until much later that the barrel's battered remains floated out into the mist. Attached was Charles' right arm, still strapped down, with his tattoo visible: "Don't Forget Me Annie."

Reference: infoniagara.com

The Daredevils of Niagara Falls:
www.DarwinAwards.com/book/niagara.html

Darwin Award: Hurricane Blumpkin

Confirmed by Darwin

19 September 2003, Virginia

Hurricane Isabel whipped shallow creeks into raging rivers, before calming down to a violent tropical storm. What better time for a canoe trip? Especially at two-thirty in the morning, on a moonless night? Enter "Blumpkin," twenty-one, captain of the James Madison University rugby team, described as "insane, just indestructible."

He left his own party with friends who "thought it would be all ha, ha and funny" to take the canoe straight down Blacks Run Stream to Blumpkin's old house.

Winds were gusting to fifty miles per hour, as nearly a foot of rain fell on the Shenandoah Valley. The Boy Scout canoe merit badge says, "If in doubt . . . survey the water from shore. Do not run any but the mildest rapids unless you have a guide who knows the river. Wear life jackets in all rough water." Surely Blumpkin noticed that the knee-deep water of Blacks Run was now a flood churning higher than his head. Nevertheless, he launched—and just as quickly capsized. The boat occupants were tossed into the swift, storm-fed stream.

Our "indestructible" friend Blumpkin was sucked underwater twice, to resurface at dawn, one hundred yards downstream, with a Darwin Award clutched in his fist. His female companion managed to reach shore, as did his male companion, who knew it "wasn't a good idea from the start."

Reference: www.wina.com, *Daily News-Record, The Breeze*

DARWIN AWARD:
A CLOSER LOOK AT VICTORIA FALLS
Confirmed by Darwin
31 DECEMBER 2004, ZIMBABWE

The one-hundred-year-old Victoria Falls Bridge, linking Zimbabwe and Zambia, offers a spectacular view of the eighty-meter chasm. Continuous spray from the massive waterfall makes the rocks and vegetation along the lip as slippery as a slide at a water park, but far less tolerant of error.

While taking pictures at the falls with his girlfriend on New Year's Eve, Michael, fifty, dropped his spectacles over the rim. He would hardly be able to enjoy the view without them, so he decided to retrieve them.

He was intelligent enough to be aware of the risk. Headmaster at Summit College in Johannesburg and a highly regarded lecturer at geography conferences, he knew how to assess the physical world. Edging out on the slick rim, reaching toward his glasses, he slipped—and fell forty meters to his death. His body was recovered by helicopter.

Reference: *Mail & Guardian*

HONORABLE MENTION: CATCHING THE BOAT

Confirmed by Darwin

28 SEPTEMBER 2003, VANCOUVER, CANADA

Isaac, a thirty-six-year-old carpenter, had a brilliant plan to become a stunt man. During the Vancouver Film Festival, he would bungee jump from the Lions Gate Bridge, gracefully descend to the deck of a passing cruise ship, and disengage from the bungee cable as smoothly as James Bond, to the awe of the passengers. Producers and movie people who had jetted in from all over the world would marvel at his work. Over cocktails, they would compete to hire him for their next film.

Stunt men work with stunt coordinators, who carefully plot out each acrobatic feat. But Isaac was a do-it-yourself man. He planned for over two years, checking the height of the tides, boat schedules, and deck layouts. He even lined up sponsors and recruited assistants. But as it turned out, he would have been better off hiring a stunt coordinator.

The jump began perfectly. Isaac took a swan dive off the bridge, trailing the bungee cord behind him. He felt it grow taut as it stretched and began to slow his descent. The tennis court of the cruise ship drew nearer . . . and nearer . . .

. . . and nearer, until he banged into the deck, vectored into a volleyball net, bounced against a deck railing, and found himself flying once more into the air, watching the cruise ship sail away.

Isaac failed to make his James Bond entrance, but "people on the boat loved it," he said. "They were screaming, yelling, waving." A witness, however, described the reaction as "shrieks of horror."

Isaac dangled above the water, confirming that no bones were broken and making a mental note to use a shorter bungee cord next time. A water taxi positioned itself beneath him, and he descended to its deck and disengaged from the bungee cable . . . to a less than appreciative audience. He was turned over to the police, who charged him with criminal mischief.

He is still waiting to hear from the movie producers.

Reference: AP, cnn.com

HONORABLE MENTION: GO WITH THE FLOE

Confirmed by Darwin
6 APRIL 2003, QUEBEC, CANADA

Elbert, described as a "woodsman," was previously nominated for an Honorable Mention for trying to adopt a bear cub as a pet. He stole "Buddy Bear" from its snarling mother and dragged it behind his Jet Ski to subdue it. Quebec, the only Canadian province with no animal-protection laws, was unable to prosecute Elbert for that incident. But in a karmic inevitability, he was soon in the spotlight once again.

During the spring thaw, Elbert found himself fascinated by the ice floes drifting rapidly down the Gatineau River near Ottawa. Shortly thereafter, a downstream resident was cleaning her car, "when someone ran up to report a man floating downriver on a little piece of ice." That man, of course, was Elbert. "After we called 911 we went to watch. He was traveling pretty quick because the water is fast."

Elbert's impulsive ride ended where the ice floes piled up on a hydro-boom strung across the river, above a set of rapids. This left him stranded on a fifteen-foot cake of ice in the middle of the frosty Gatineau River. Two young men in a rowboat rescued our adventurer, thereby preventing him from capturing a Darwin Award that day.

When police asked him what he was thinking, Elbert said, "I just felt like going for a ride."

Reference: *Low Down to Hull and Back News,* www.snowgoer.com

PERSONAL ACCOUNT: DO-IT-YOURSELF BASS BOAT
SEPTEMBER 2004, ARKANSAS

My son is a rescue diver with the sheriff's department. About two months ago, they were called out for an emergency rescue of several people who had fallen in the water after their boat had tipped over.

When the rescue team arrived at the scene, other boaters had pulled two men out of the water. Two other cloth-covered items were floating ominously in the river. But when the divers entered the water, they were relieved to discover that these were not bodies.

The story was that the two rescued men had decided to do a little fishing. Bass fishermen spend tens of thousands of dollars outfitting their specialized boats with fancy electronic fish finders and other gear, and they sometimes make the boats into floating palaces, with reclining seats that allow them to relax while they're waiting for the Big One to strike. But not everyone can afford the best.

These two fishermen had to make do with a fourteen-foot, flat-bottom jon boat. Wanting to be comfortable, and not having the money for a real bass boat, these two dim bulbs decided to put a couple of La-Z-Boy recliners on their skiff. They must have barely had enough room left for their supply of beer. Needless to say, they both decided to recline at the same time, and you can figure out the rest of the story.

My son said that he and the rest of the rescue team were laughing so hard that they could hardly do their job.

Reference: Mark Goecke, Personal Account

CHAPTER 3

Women

Few women win Darwin Awards, but this book is lucky enough to have a strong selection of female applicants. We have a spy, two explosions, pilot sex and street sex, a desperate smoker, a gymnast, an amateur mechanic, and a thief. We also have a Jet Ski, a hurricane, a raging river, a roller coaster, gasoline, and an aerosol can. But first, an essay on the damage that females do to their mates. . . .

Discussion: Love Bites

Annaliese Beery, Science Writer

When humans get themselves killed in creative ways, they are usually considered unfit individuals. But for some species, self-sacrifice of the ultimate kind is a common, adaptive part of mating. The process is called sexual cannibalism, and it's every bit as gory as it sounds.

You probably know that black widow females sometimes consume their mates (along with 95 percent of their young) and many species, from crickets to scorpions, indulge similarly cannibalistic appetites after sex. One fly, *Serromyia femorata,* administers a death kiss, sucking the body of her mate through his mouth as a post-copulatory snack. But the masochism prize in the mating game goes to the suitor of another poisonous widow, the Australian redback spider *Lactodectus hasselti.* He actually tries to feed himself to his partner.

Before mating can begin, the male redback spider must go through a few preparations. First he spins a special web and deposits sperm on it. Then he sucks the sperm packets into his pedipalps, two appendages on the front of his head that he might otherwise use to hold food. Once he's primed and ready, this inconspicuous brown male searches for the rare web containing the irresistible black and red female, who is fifty times his weight.

The drama begins in the standard spider mating position: He stands on her large abdomen and inserts a palp into one of her genital openings. But then the redback male does something different. He uses his palp as a pivot to somersault 180 degrees and land on the female's jaws. The female may then pierce his abdomen and inject enzymes, beginning the digestion process. The male is ready for this outcome—he hopes for it—and his abdomen is compartmentalized to slow his demise. Often he will manage to insert his other palp in her second genital opening, then leap into her jaws again. Eventually he is devoured, mating all the while. If he survives his daring leaps, it is only because the female isn't hungry. (She is typically ravenous.)

Other male widow spiders don't feed themselves to their mates. So what drives the male redback to such lengths? In the lingo of evolutionary biologists, "What's in it for him?" Scientist Maydianne Andrade of the University of Toronto performed an experiment to find out: She mated redback spiders in the lab and determined how many eggs males fertilized when they were eaten—or spared. After a first pairing the females were allowed to mate again. Dr. Andrade found that when the first male was eaten, the female mated with him for twice as long (while eating him), and the "male meal" fertilized roughly twice as many eggs as an uneaten male. She was also much less likely to mate again with a second male. The male fertilizes more eggs, which is the goal.

But is it worth it for a male to lose the chance to mate again? For the male redback spider, the answer is yes. He only lives eight weeks, compared to the female redback's two-year

lifespan. Only 20 percent of males ever find one female, let alone two. Even if a redback male did get lucky twice, he would be functionally sterile, because his palps are damaged during mating and emptied of sperm. Cannibalized, the male doubles his "paternity benefits"—offspring. The female he inseminated can store his sperm for the rest of her life, potentially producing thousands of offspring. Generation after generation, this paternity advantage has cemented risky behavior in males. Each suitor performs the same suicidal somersault, trading his life for more offspring.

Widow spiders aren't the only animals with a penchant for cannibalism. Several species of praying mantis also eat their mates. Mantises are aggressive hunters, occasionally catching much larger prey, including hummingbirds. (One biologist often says the only thing mantises pray for is a good meal.) Most species only cannibalize mates regularly in captivity, but one species in particular deserves its bloodthirsty reputation. The European Mantis (*Mantis religiosa*) is a common, two- to three-inch green mantis with an uncommon appetite. In the wild, the female eats a third of her partners. She eats even more in the lab when the males can't escape. She is so voracious that the male European mantis forgoes mating displays in favor of surprise. No foreplay for her! He sneaks up on the female from behind, so she won't get any ideas about his juicy head. If he can get close enough, he'll leap onto her back and begin to mate.

If the female spots her mate's head during the process, she'll snatch it and begin to dine. The decapitated male only has one goal at this unfortunate juncture. He thrashes wildly, and though headless, manages to mate with her. Mantis females eat all parts of the male they can reach. At least the male redback spider's death is voluntary. Cannibalism in the European mantis shows no sign of male buy-in. He makes a tremendous effort to avoid being eaten, his wariness a good indication that sexual cannibalism has shaped the evolution of his behavior.

Sexual cannibalism may be rare and extreme, but it has evolved several times in the animal kingdom. For species like the redback spider and the European mantis, reproduction trumps even death. It always does—natural selection ensures that the fittest genes are perpetuated, even when the process is painful for the participants. So when the male redback spider gives his life as a snack, he can honestly claim: "my genes made me do it."

Further reading:

Andrade, M.C.B. 2003. "Risky mate search and male self-sacrifice in redback spiders." *Behavioral Ecology,* 14: 531–538.

Lawrence, S.E. 1992. "Sexual cannibalism in the praying mantid, *Mantis religiosa*: a field study." *Animal Behavior,* 43: 569–583.

Johns, P.M., and Maxwell, M.R. 1997. "Sexual cannibalism: who benefits?" *Trends in Ecology and Evolution,* 12(4): 127–128.

Additional References:

Andrade, M.C.B., and Banta, E.M. 2002. "Value of remating and functional sterility in redback spiders." *Animal Behavior,* 63: 857–870.

Andrade, M.C.B. 1996. "Sexual selection for male sacrifice in the Australian redback spider." *Science,* 271: 70–72.

Mukerjee, M. October 1995. "Giving your all." *Scientific American.*

Now that we've read about the deadly dangers that female insects pose to their males, let's turn the tables, and watch female humans place themselves in equally deadly predicaments. It is with great pleasure that I introduce these stories about feminine wiles. . . .

Video of the male redback spider's suicidal somersault:

www.DarwinAwards.com/book/spider.html

Darwin Award: Military Intelligence

Unconfirmed by Darwin

1970s, Northern Ireland

Back in the late seventies, intelligence units in Northern Ireland were issued exploding briefcases to carry sensitive documents. These briefcases were lined with oxygen bricks. To arm the case, one simply removed a small pin next to the handle of the case. Thus armed, an opened case would instantly combust, destroying everything within a meter of it.

Because there was a half-second delay before the bricks ignited, the lids were designed to stop on a spring catch, so that no document could be rescued or photographed before it was destroyed.

To open the case safely, therefore, the sequence was:

1. Make sure the arming pin is in place.
2. Open the case.
3. Using a thin object such as a ruler, push back the spring catch.
4. The case will now open.

But in this particular case, the sequence went as follows:

1. Make sure the arming pin is in place.
2. Open the case.
3. Look for a small thin object to push back the catch.
4. Find none immediately available.
5. Notice that the arming pin is a small thin object.
6. Use the arming pin to push back the catch.
7. Kiss one "intelligence" unit goodbye.

Reference: Eyewitness account, verification sought

DARWIN AWARD: MILE HIGH CLUB FAILURE

Confirmed by Darwin

23 DECEMBER 1991, FLORIDA

This account of an aircraft accident is quoted directly from the National Transportation Safety Board report, with comments added in brackets for clarity.

Aircraft: Piper PA-34-200T, Registration: N47506

Injuries: 2 Fatal.

The private pilot and a pilot-rated passenger [two pilots] were going to practice simulated instrument flight. Witnesses observed the airplane's right wing fail in a dive and crash. Examination of the wreckage and bodies revealed that both occupants were partially clothed and the front right seat was in the full aft reclining position. [The pilots had converted the copilot seat to a bed.] Neither body showed evidence of seat belts or shoulder harnesses being worn. [They were lying on the bed.] Examination of the individuals' clothing revealed no evidence of ripping or distress to the zippers and belts. [Their lack of clothing seemed to be voluntary.]

The National Transportation Safety Board determines the probable cause(s) of this accident as follows:

The pilot in command's improper in-flight decision to divert her attention to other activities not related to the conduct of the flight. [The pilot and copilot were having sex, and nobody was flying the plane.] Contributing to the accident was the exceeding of the design limits of the airplane leading to a wing failure.

[Lack of a pilot caused the plane to fly erratically, overstressing the wing and leading to a crash.]

Reference: NTSB #MIA92FA051

> **READER COMMENTS:**
>
> "Get an autopilot!"
>
> "The ultimate high!"
>
> "I guess they <u>did</u> give a flying f——."
>
> "Perhaps Durex ought to sell parachutes as well. . . ."
>
> "Well, obviously they were erotic . . . oh, oops, I mean erratic, pilots."

DARWIN AWARD: ULTIMATE QUEST FOR AIRTIME

Confirmed by Darwin

31 MAY 2003, INDIANA

Tamar came all the way from New York for the annual Stark Raven Mad event at the Splashin' Safari water park at Holiday World, where members of the American Coaster Enthusiasts planned a rendezvous on Memorial Day weekend. The thirty-two-year-old eagerly looked forward to riding the Raven, later described by Spencer County Prosecutor Jon Dartt as "one of the world's most terrifying roller coasters."

Tamar planned what coaster enthusiasts call "catching airtime," standing up during the ride to show bravery. The park staff warned the "spirited and intelligent" Harvard MBA, along with the rest of the group, "Don't mess with our safety equipment." Tamar's seat belt and lap-bar restraint were in place when the train left the station. But you can't catch airtime that way. Her seat belt was later found unbuckled and tucked into the seat cushions.

As the train swooped over the precipice into the "infamous drop" on the fifth turn at sixty miles per hour, where the g-forces are notoriously skyward, Tamar apparently unlatched her seat belt and stood up. The train dropped, but Tamar didn't. She caught good air until she landed on the ground, sixty-nine feet below.

Reference: *New York Daily News, Coaster Buzz*

DARWIN AWARD: RIGHT OVER THE DAM

Confirmed by Darwin

24 JULY 2004, WISCONSIN

Barbara, twenty-six, must have listened too many times to the old song "High Hopes" and its verse about a perky little fish: "And she swam, and she swam right over the dam." But Barbara needed more than willpower to fulfill her high hopes when she decided to take the shortest route between the Upper Dells and the Lower Dells.

She piloted a personal watercraft at high speed past numerous signs warning craft to slow down because of the imminent danger. She wove through the support posts of two separate bridges, one for trains, and one for cars. She ignored the screaming pleas of her twenty-four-year-old passenger, who finally jumped off at the last minute. And she did it—she soared over that dam like a flying fish.

Then she crash-landed on the concrete spillway, dying instantly.

Nearby residents told police that Barbara had been speeding like a maniac at high speeds in no-wake zones near the shore, despite the many posted warnings. Blood tests showed she had also been drinking like a fish. When asked to comment on her demise, the police chief said, "It kind of speaks for itself."

Reference: *Wisconsin Dells Events*

DARWIN AWARD: LOVE STRUCK
Confirmed by Darwin

3 MARCH 2002, ENGLAND

*"Does it really matter what these affectionate
people do, so long as they don't do it in the street
and frighten the horses?"*

—Mrs. Patrick Campbell

As Kim and Paul left the Sheffield pub, they noticed that a street-light was burned out, creating a pool of darkness on the road. Unable to rein in their passion, they began to consummate their relationship on the asphalt outside the pub. Witnesses said the couple was lying right on the white line, kissing and cuddling.

The passionate pair were warned of the danger of their coital position not once, not twice, but three times—by a car driver, a bus driver, and a pedestrian. An off-duty paramedic honked and shouted, "You want to get up, otherwise you'll be run over." The man simply said "Cheers, mate," and the paramedic heard a female laughing. A bus driver swerved to avoid them, and drove past with wheels on the curb. A concerned pedestrian shouted to warn them that another bus was headed their way.

Despite these disruptions, Kim and Paul continued, oblivious to the approach of a small, single-decker Nipper bus. The bus driver mistook the undulating shape for a bag of rubbish in the poorly lit street, and was unable to stop in time. There was a dull thud . . .

Kim and Paul were struck and killed at midnight. Paramedics found Kim lying on her back with her jumper pulled up, and Paul between her legs with his trousers pulled down.

The only downside to this timely removal of lunacy from the gene pool is the fate of the bus driver. Despite the couple's irregular actions, and a police investigator's statement that "to expect a driver to anticipate a pedestrian lying in the road is out of the ordinary," a judge fined him for careless driving, and his license was revoked for six months. Fortunately, his employers consider him an excellent employee, and plan to give him other duties. Relatives of the victims said they were glad the driver had kept his job.

This tale surely answers the Beatles' question, *"Why don't we do it in the road?"*

Reference: The Sun Online, *Daily Sport* (UK), www.sundaytimes.co.za, *Sheffield Star*, www.yorkshiretv.com, *Yorkshire Post*

DARWIN AWARD: HURRICANE NEWS JUNKIE
Unconfirmed by Darwin
3 DECEMBER 1999, DENMARK

A powerful winter storm system plowed through Europe. Hurricane-force winds gusted to one hundred ten miles per hour, and massive waves pounded the seashore. One woman was anxiously watching news of "the worst storm in Denmark this century" when the TV picture suddenly became too grainy to see. The antenna on the roof had come loose and started to bang around.

Determined not to miss any information, and despite the howling winds, she decided to climb up on the roof to fix the antenna. She was blown off the roof by the hurricane winds and killed. As a consolation prize, she became a major part of the news over the next few days.

Reference (hurricane only): Numerous news articles

DARWIN AWARD: DYING FOR A CIGGIE

Confirmed by Darwin

17 JUNE 2003, UNITED KINGDOM

National Express runs bus services throughout the U.K. The service between Aberdeen and London takes approximately twelve hours. There's no smoking on the coach, making it a long trip for addicts. Sandra, forty-three, was riding south from Glasgow to visit her family, and she was getting more and more desperate for a cigarette.

The coach stopped at Carlisle. Finally she could satisfy her craving! But no, she was not allowed to get off the coach. Sandra sat in the bus, becoming more agitated by the mile. She was craving a cigarette. She needed it—now.

Fellow passengers said she became increasingly anxious as the journey continued, and started shouting that she wanted to get off. However, the coach was on a motorway at the time and was not allowed to stop except for an emergency. They saw Sandra push her hands against the passenger door in the middle of the lower deck. Surely she couldn't be trying to get off the coach to have that cigarette she'd been dreaming of, could she?

Oh, yes she could!

Police concluded that she fell out of the coach, which was traveling at approximately sixty miles per hour, and was crushed under its wheels. At that point, the coach made that hoped-for emergency stop, but it was too late for Sandra. She never did get to enjoy that cigarette.

Reference: BBC News

DARWIN AWARD: OFF-ROAD DRIVING

Confirmed by Darwin

6 JANUARY 2005, JOHANNESBURG, SOUTH AFRICA

Massive thunderstorms had turned the Braamfontein Spruit into a raging river. It was a little past midnight when police warned Barbara, thirty-three, that a flash flood was inundating the bridge ahead. They urged her not to cross. But Barbara was driving a BMW X3, an off-road vehicle with xDrive all-wheel-drive.

Brochures assured her that the luxury SUV with Sensatec upholstery and an eight-speaker stereo system had "virtually unlimited agility." So Barbara laughed off the police advice and continued toward the bridge. The xDrive all-wheel-drive lost its grip as the floodwaters swept her BMW X3 off the bridge. Her body was found later inside the vehicle more than a mile down the river.

Reference: *Mail & Guardian*

DARWIN AWARD: WHAT I CAN STILL DO

Confirmed by Darwin

16 JANUARY 2005, FORT MYERS, FLORIDA

Two North Fort Myers residents, twenty-three-year-old Molly and her husband, had rented a room in a local motel for some unspecified activity, perhaps involving perpetuation of the species. As Molly entered the second-floor room, she went straight for the lanai, which overlooked a concrete patio. Most guests would have seen the railing on the edge of the lanai as a safety feature, but for Molly it brought to mind fond memories of her youthful gymnastic abilities.

Molly called out, "Watch to see what I can still do." These would be her last words. She did a flip onto the railing for a handstand, just the way she used to do, but then toppled over the other side, slamming into the patio fifteen feet below. She was pronounced dead at the hospital.

Reference: *Fort Myers News-Press*, AP

HONORABLE MENTION: A FAST ESCAPE

Confirmed by Darwin

5 JANUARY 2004, NEW YORK, NEW YORK

Security guards caught a nineteen-year-old woman who had been sneaking into offices, stealing wallets out of coat pockets. The guards locked her in a room on the tenth floor and waited for police to arrive.

The woman was desperate to escape. There was no way she could get past the guards outside the door. But she was in luck—the window opened! She climbed onto the ledge, and she was free!

Far below, traffic whizzed by on 42nd Street. Was she startled by the security guards coming back into the room? Or caught off-balance by a wayward pigeon? Or hoping to win a Darwin Award? She's not telling, but she fell or jumped from the ledge, landing on scaffolding eight stories below.

She lost her bid for a full Darwin, surviving the fall with several broken bones. But her escape was only temporary. She was arrested and charged with burglary before being taken to a hospital in critical condition.

Personal Account: Gas Spill

1993, Pittsburgh, Pennsylvania

I will be the first to admit that this only qualifies as an Honorable Mention—but how many people get the *prosecution* to request a mental competency hearing?

In Pittsburgh, my roommate's coworker was gassing up her car. The automatic shutoff didn't engage, so when the tank was full, a little gas overflowed. When she realized this, she declared that she wasn't paying for gas on the ground—she would only pay for what was in her car. The attendant stated that she had to pay for all the gas she had pumped. She reiterated that not all of it went into her car.

She then said, "Watch, I'll prove it."

Prove it she did. She threw her *lit* cigarette on the ground where the gas spilled. The puddle ignited! Fortunately, they were able to put out the fire before anything worse happened.

She was arrested for inciting a catastrophe. While listening to the testimony at her preliminary hearing, the prosecutor stated, "That's crazy. That's insane!" The defense attorney—either spotting a good line of defense, or agreeing with the prosecutor—asked, "Are you going to request a psychiatric evaluation?" To which the prosecutor replied, "You damn betcha."

Reference: Personal Account

PERSONAL ACCOUNT: STUPID CAR
SUMMER 2003, OREGON

There was no media coverage on this one. I was a witness and rescuer. Around seven A.M., I looked up from the machine I was operating at work and saw an older Nissan at the stop sign across the street. Its emergency flashers were on. A heavyset young woman emerged, opened the hood, and leaned in to manipulate something inside. Suddenly the car lurched forward, knocking her down.

I immediately ran for the door. By the time I started across the parking lot, the bumper of the car was slowly shoving her out into the four-lane boulevard! The situation reminded me of the Stephen King story where the car starts trying to kill people. Unsuccessful at crushing her, the woman's car was pushing her into the boulevard's right lane, where other cars could finish the job.

After checking for traffic, I ran across the street to help. Very fortunately for her, the driver of the next vehicle to approach her (a school bus) was quick-witted enough to turn on the flashing red lights, stopping traffic.

As I sprinted to the driver's door, I remember feeling a flash of irritation as the woman gasped to me, "Put it in reverse." Did she think I was going to try to lift it off her? I hopped in and carefully reversed the car. She stood up, brushed herself off, and said, "Stupid car. The transmission linkage is always sticking."

Dumbfounded, all I could think of to say was, "Maybe you should set the parking brake next time." I consciously didn't say, "The *car* is stupid?"

Reference: John A Hancock, Personal Account

PERSONAL ACCOUNT: AIR FRESHENER
1983, UK

Young Mick had settled in for a good night's sleep when he was awakened by a loud explosion. His bedroom door had been blown open by air pressure, and his curtains had flown out the open window. He rushed downstairs to find his mother staggering from the kitchen with smoke rising from patches where there used to be hair. She seemed more dazed than injured, so he sat her down and went into the kitchen.

It looked like a small bomb had gone off. The net curtains were a pile of melted nylon, and the cotton curtains were still on fire. Mick put them out with a few glasses of water and returned to his mother to find out what had happened.

"Well," she said, "I thought that the kitchen was a little smelly so I got out a spray can of air freshener. Nothing came out but I knew something was inside, because I could hear it when I shook the can. So I thought I'd open it with the can opener and sprinkle some of the contents around."

Propellant spurted from the can as soon as the can opener cut into it, startling Mom and causing her to throw the can into the air. It landed on the gas stove, where the pilot light instantly turned the can into a fireball. Mom had narrowly avoided winning herself a Darwin Award.

In positive psychology terms, Mom was conditioning her son to react to danger and avoid his own untimely removal from the gene pool. Mom's lesson worked. Mick is still alive and passing on her lessons to the rest of us.

Reference: Mick, Personal Account

In another lesson, Mick's mother showed him a broken vacuum cleaner. She had tugged too hard on the power cord and pulled the wires loose. "I opened the plug and put the wires back," she said, "but it still doesn't work." Mick opened the plug to find all three wires twisted together and inserted, luckily, into the neutral pin. If she had chosen the live pin, the vacuum cleaner would have become electrified, waiting for Mom to touch it and send two hundred forty volts charging through her on their way to ground.

CHAPTER 4

Animals

An animal might win a Darwin Award if it migrated in the wrong direction. But in this chapter, animals are not the winners; they are the backdrop against which humans lose to Mother Nature. Before we get into the elephants, snakes, raccoons, chickens, bees, bugs, birds, eels, sharks, toads, horses, and bison—first, an essay on our cousin, the chimpanzee.

DISCUSSION:
"BROTHER, CAN YOU SPARE A BANANA?"

James G. Petropoulos, Science Writer

One may well ask that question of the next chimpanzee one meets. Recent research shows that humans (*Homo sapiens*) and chimpanzees (*Pan troglodytes*) are 99.4% genetically compatible, although (based on fossil and genetic evidence) the two species diverged five to seven million years ago. So close are the similarities that it has been suggested that chimpanzees be reclassified as genus Homo. Yet it is clear that chimpanzees and humans are physically and mentally quite different. Of the great apes, the chimpanzee is by far our closest relative. The gorilla is less closely related, and the orangutan (despite it's almost human face) even less so. Genetic research on all four species is beginning to yield information on what exactly makes humans different, and in time, perhaps will shed light on what makes us human.

A look at the physical differences between chimps and humans helps illustrate these minor genetic differences. Chimpanzees are arboreal; though omnivorous, they live on a diet consisting chiefly of fruit; they are four to seven times as strong as humans; they are more agile but less dexterous than humans. Humans, of course, are bipedal, very much omnivorous, predatory by instinct, and have superior intellect and communication skills. It has been proposed that the genetic differences between chimpanzees and humans are largely due to the two species' differing lifestyles, which can perhaps explain why, after five to seven million years, chimpanzees still live in trees and humans do not.

The most easily recognizable genetic difference between humans and chimpanzees is the number of chromosome pairs. Humans have twenty-three pairs, chimpanzees have twenty-four. However, this difference is deceptive. Findings suggest that somewhere along the course of human evolution, two pairs of "chimp" chromosomes fused and rearranged themselves into our familiar twenty-three. The genetic information contained in those "fused" chromosomes has both human and ape counterparts.

The genetic differences scientists are concentrating on may surprise many readers.

Andrew G. Clark of Cornell University recently completed the most comprehensive comparison study to date of the genetic differences between humans and chimpanzees. Using a supercomputer, a partial chimpanzee DNA map of eighteen million sequences was lined up with the genomes of a human and a mouse, to determine which human genes were evolving most quickly. It was hypothesized that if natural selection favored certain genes, perhaps these genes were part of what made us "human." Starting with 23,000 genes, the final field was whittled down to 7,645 human genes that most differed from chimpanzees and mice. Clark and his team isolated genes that determine sense of smell, digestion of protein, development of long bones, hairiness, and hearing. Clark's

conclusions were that at some point, human olfactory senses and amino-acid metabolism genetically diverged from those of the chimpanzee, presumably enabling early humans to better smell the types of food they sought, and to better process the proteins found therein. These findings coincide with archaeological evidence that humans began eating meat about two million years ago. These genetic mutations may have been brought about by a new ecological niche created by climate changes.

The genes that determine amino-acid metabolism explain why we are able to digest more dietary proteins, and also lend a clue as to what may have resulted when this newfound digestive ability triggered changes in other proteins. Findings published by the RIKEN Genomic Sciences Centre in Japan support the hypothesis that certain proteins (for example, those affecting brain tissue) may have been genetically altered over time by our change to a more carnivorous diet. As man began chemically altering his food by cooking it and adding other proteins to his diet, such as dairy and legumes, further changes in human proteins may have been triggered, resulting in modern humans.

Another discovery was made by the Howard Hughes Medical Institute. A gene known as ASPM was isolated. Mutations in ASPM affect the size of the cerebral cortex, the part of the brain most closely associated with our "humanity." This protein is much more complex in human form than in apes, and might be a key factor in the evolution of the large human brain.

Clark speculated that genes connected with the sense of hearing might also have contributed to the divergence between humans and chimpanzees, and that these genes may be at the root of human language and communicative ability. He concluded, "Perhaps some of the genes that enable humans to understand speech [involve] not only the brain, but also hearing."

One such gene, alpha-tectorin, determines the makeup of the tectorial membrane of the inner ear. It is known that mutations in this gene cause congenital deafness in humans; perhaps the fine-tuning of alpha-tectorin millions of years ago enabled early humans to understand more complex speech. The difficulty in training chimpanzees to understand human language suggests that perhaps their hearing isn't quite as acute as our own. Our advanced ability to communicate—very much a part of our humanity—may all be due to a gene acting upon an obscure ear protein!

Clark warns, however, that the biological differences between humans and chimpanzees are not necessarily the result of one or even many particular genes, but the hypotheses raised by his experiment certainly merit further study.

Seemingly minor differences in our genetic makeup have resulted in two very different critters, and science is only now beginning to sort it all out. There are yet other differences. Chimpanzees are more genetically diverse than humans; among humans, those living in Africa are more genetically diverse than non-Africans. One theory is that all humans living today sprang from a single female ancestor living in Africa some two hundred thousand years ago. This theory is based not on nuclear DNA, but on mitochondrial DNA. This is another story for another day, but we can be sure that the 1 percent difference between humans and chimpanzees is more astonishing than the 99 percent similarity.

So go ahead and ask a brother chimp if he can spare a banana . . . chances are he'll have no idea what you're talking about!

References:

Cornell News, December 18, 2003

University of Chicago Hospitals article, "Human Brain Still Evolving," September 8, 2005

Wikipedia.com, article on "Mitochondrial Eve"

Wildman et al. "Genomics in Humans and Chimpanzees"

Now that we've developed a fellow feel for the apes, enjoy these stories about other members of the animal kingdom that have the misfortune to share the planet with *Homo sapiens clueless*.

DARWIN AWARD: MINING FOR ELEPHANTS

Confirmed by Darwin

15 FEBRUARY 2005, ZIMBABWE

The elephants were trampling Christian's maize field, which he had planted on an elephant trail of long standing. He had to find a way to fight back! Fortunately, there was an old minefield nearby, on the Zimbabwe-Mozambique border. Christian figured a few land mines planted around his field would soon teach the elephants a lesson they would never forget.

Christian may have gotten the idea of using the mines from a couple of incidents that had recently transpired. A local resident had been injured after picking up a land mine while herding cattle the week before. A week before that, another Rushinga man had lost part of his leg after stepping on a land mine. The other villagers saw the writing on the wall, and avoided the mines.

But Christian realized they were just what he needed. Clearly, these mines could cause great damage to an elephant! He dug up five that had been exposed by recent heavy rains. And as he carried them home, the unstable mines detonated, killing Christian instantly.

The total number of elephants injured? Zero.

Reference: *Zimbabwe Herald*

DARWIN AWARD: SNAKE MAN
Confirmed by Darwin
19 MARCH 2004, SI SA KET PROVINCE, THAILAND

During his snake-handling performance, Boonreung the "Snake Man" was bitten on the right elbow by a deadly mamba. While a lesser mortal might have rushed to a doctor for a dose of antivenin, the daring thirty-four-year-old had his own treatment method: He downed a shot of whiskey and some herbal medicine. But alcohol and herbs are not generally recognized as effective against snakebites. It was on with the show—until paralysis gradually took hold, and he collapsed.

At this point, he was unable to speak, and thus raised no objections as bystanders took him to Praibung Hospital. But it was too late. The poison had spread throughout his body, and he died the same day. Ironically, Boonreung is immortalized in the *Guinness Book of World Records* for having spent seven days in a roomful of venomous snakes in 1998.

Reference: AP Asia

The mamba's bite was described by Jack Seale, owner of a snake and animal park near Johannesburg, as "a pure neurotoxin—it gives you a buzz." The victim becomes lightheaded, tingly, and warm. "It's a lovely feeling," says Seale. A single bite can deliver four hundred milligrams of paralyzing venom; a mere ten milligrams can be fatal to a human. When Seale was bitten, his treatment consisted of injections of antivenin, cortisone, and adrenalin, which helped him survive long enough to be hooked up to a heart-lung machine. After a week of dialysis and blood transfusions, he could finally wiggle a single finger. ("Black Mamba!" International Wildlife, Nov/Dec 1996.)

DARWIN AWARD: ELEPHANT TAIL

Confirmed by Darwin

28 JANUARY 2005, PENDANG, THAILAND

It's no secret that elephants are big. Elephants eat hundreds of pounds of food a day just to maintain their weight. Indian elephants are nine feet tall at the shoulder. They're so powerful that in Southeast Asia, males are used to haul massive tree trunks with their three-foot tusks, work performed by heavy equipment in other countries.

It's also no secret that teasing an animal makes it mad. Teasing an animal that can carry a tree with its tusks may not be a good idea. Yet that was the very idea that formed in Prawat's head when he saw a herd of five performing elephants chained to trees outside a Buddhist temple.

While the owner waited inside for an entertainment permit, Prawat, a fifty-year-old rubber-tapper, offered sugar cane to one of the ever-hungry elephants . . . then pulled it away. Then he did it again. And again. And again.

The game was great fun for Prawat, but the elephant quickly tired of it. The last time Prawat withdrew the treat, the elephant swung his massive tusks and gored him through the stomach. Prawat died on the way to the hospital. The elephant got his treat.

Reference: *The Star* (Kuala Lumpur)

DARWIN AWARD: "HAZARD BEFELL HIM"
Confirmed by Darwin
27 MARCH 1981, INDIANA

Late one March evening, Bruce awoke at the foot of a utility pole in the woods, his dog asleep by his side and a crispy, dead raccoon nearby. Bruce was alarmed to discover "severe burns on his forearms, hands, and genitals, necessitating their amputation."

What happened? The details came out in court, when Bruce sued the utility company for removing him from the gene pool.

He had been out coon hunting when his dog caught the scent and chased a raccoon up a power pole. The raccoon perched on a glass insulator. Bruce was prepared for just such an event. He strapped his trusty steel pole climbers to his boots, and made his way up the pole. . . .

The court found Bruce contributory negligent, stating succinctly, "It [is] clear that, in climbing the utility pole, slapping and squalling at the raccoon, thereby agitating it when it was perilously close to charged wires, Bruce should have appreciated the hazard that ultimately befell him."

Reference: 1986 Ind. App. LEXIS 3134

DARWIN AWARD: CHICKEN TO GO

Confirmed by Darwin

3 OCTOBER 2004, ROMANIA

Radu, sixty-seven, lived in a formerly peaceful village near Galati. But lately Radu couldn't get any sleep, all because of a single noisy chicken. Night after night he dreamed of wringing its neck, or even better, chopping its head off and eating it. One night, he finally had enough. He roused himself from bed and headed out to the yard in his underwear, determined to bring silence to his home.

The sleep-deprived villager grabbed that noisy chicken by the neck and chopped its head right off. Only then did he realize that he had confused his own penis for the chicken's neck. While Radu stood stunned by his folly, his dog rushed over and gobbled up the treat.

He was rushed to the hospital, bleeding heavily. Doctors sewed up the wound and pronounced him out of danger. He is also in no danger of reproducing.

Reference: Reuters

DARWIN AWARD: A HONEY OF A BUZZ

Confirmed by Darwin
SEPTEMBER 2003, MEXICO

An unidentified sixty-year-old Escobedo man was still thirsty after drinking what most would consider "too much alcohol." He stumbled toward a nearby beehive, hoping to follow the beer with a bit of honey.

He thought the bees would surely share. Instead, they obeyed a Darwinian signal bred into them for millennia. More than a thousand noble fighters gave their all, sacrificed their stingers and their lives to protect the hive. The man, quite reasonably, responded with terminal anaphylactic shock.

A hospital spokesman disputed the theory that bees had killed him, attributing his demise to "the stupid things drunken people do," and pointing out that he was otherwise healthy and would have enjoyed a long life. "The combination was lethal."

Reference: ananova.com

"Bees don't kill people, people kill bees."

HONORABLE MENTION: KILLS BUGS DEAD

Confirmed by Darwin

29 APRIL 2004, WEST VIRGINIA

Ed, sixty-three, had trouble with termites at home. He had heard that natural gas was dangerous, and figured it would be a good, low-cost way to fumigate his house. So he shut the doors and windows, turned on the gas, and spent the night in a nearby camper trailer with his wife. The next morning he stepped out of the trailer, took a breath of the crisp, cool air, and strode over to his house.

When he opened the door, the slight spark from the latch ignited the cloud of natural gas that had accumulated in his home. The force of the explosion blew him off the porch and into a nearby creek, knocked out the town's telephones and electricity, and blew the doors off a church. It rattled windows and nerves six miles away.

Ed was evacuated by helicopter to the burn unit at Cabell Huntington Hospital. His house was uninsured. It is presumed that the fumigation was effective.

Reference: West Virginia Metro News

HONORABLE MENTION: PARROT HUNTER
Confirmed by Darwin
10 APRIL 1999, FLORIDA

Bruce, eighteen, wanted a unique gift for his girlfriend, who worked as a babysitter for a neighbor's children. The neighbor thought that a Quaker parrot would be a perfect present. The beautiful green birds with gray bellies grow a foot long, counting their tails, and are worth more than $100. That was expensive, but the neighbor figured they could get a baby parrot for free . . . if they caught it.

Nothing stirs a man's blood like the thrill of the hunt. Armed with a long metal pole, Bruce set out with the neighbor and his fifteen-year-old son to reconnoiter the nesting spot of the elusive Quaker parrot. The intrepid trio may have overlooked the fact that they were trespassing on private property, and that the property was owned by Florida Power. But it is unlikely that they failed to notice that the nests in question were inside a six-foot fence topped with three rows of barbed wire, surrounding an electric substation. This 230,000-volt transformer was peppered with signs saying, DANGER HIGH VOLTAGE and NO TRESPASSING.

The hunters overcame those obstacles and entered the parrot sanctuary, where about sixty colorful birds fluttered around their large, multistory stick nests. Fortunately one of the nests was situated on a transformer low enough to interest a hunter with a seven-foot metal pole. Bruce poked at the nest hoping to dislodge a hatchling, and fifteen thousand volts of electricity found their way down the pole, through his body, and into the ground.

Bruce suffered second- and third-degree burns over 50 percent of his body. The neighbor suffered minor burns between his ankles and knees. His son was not injured.

"That's just a little hobby they have," said the neighbor's wife. "They like to go looking for those little baby Quaker parrots. I'm not saying [they were] right, but this was an accident." And all this came from an innocent question about a birthday present at a Saturday hamburger cookout!

Reference: *St. Petersburg Times*

HONORABLE MENTION: EEL ENEMA
Confirmed by Darwin
LATE 2003, HONG KONG

An unidentified fifty-year-old entered the accident and emergency department of a local hospital complaining of abdominal pain. The doctor's examination revealed peritonitis, an inflammation of the abdomen. Wondering what had caused this problem, doctors ordered an X-ray and spotted what appeared to be an eel inside his colon! Could an eel be the source of his pain?

Yes, the man admitted, there was an eel inside him. He had been suffering from constipation, he told the dubious medical staff, and thought that inserting an eel into his rectum would relieve it.

The man was rushed to the operating room, where an emergency laparoscopy disclosed that a nineteen-inch eel was biting the side of his colon. The eel also had also taken a bite out of his rectum wall in transit, so to speak. After surgeons removed the animal and reconstructed the rectum, the man's pain and constipation were both cured. He was discharged from the hospital a week later.

Reference: *Surgery,* January 2004, v. 135, p. 110

Honorable Mention: Warm Snakes

Confirmed by Darwin

4 April 1983, Washington, D.C.

Gaboon vipers are large, aggressive, ill-tempered, and among the most venomous snakes in the world. Despite these characteristics, they are normally sedentary. So it was not difficult for Lazarus, who had a penchant for snakes, to purloin two from the National Zoo. He shoved them into a plastic garbage bag, where they remained, quite docile, until Lazarus boarded a warm city bus. When the snakes warmed up, they awakened from their lethargy and realized how undesirable their new accommodations were. Naturally, they decided to move. Our sixteen-year-old herpetologist was bitten when one of the vipers ripped its fangs through the plastic bag.

> Viper venoms are <u>hemotoxic</u> (act on the blood) as compared to the neurotoxic venoms of elapids (cobras and adders). The viper family has three subfamilies: the mountain viper <u>Azemiopinae,</u> the true viper <u>Viperinae,</u> and the pit viper <u>Crotalinae.</u> They are found worldwide.
>
> <u>Introduction to Herpetology,</u> 3rd ed., Goin, Goin, and Zug, pp. 333–36.

He landed in the hospital, where antivenin serum was administered until he regained his senses. The purloined vipers were taken to the basement of the zoo's reptile house, where they were treated to a week of stress-free observation.

Reference: *Washington Post*

HONORABLE MENTION: WADES WITH SHARKS

Confirmed by Darwin

10 APRIL 2002, BAHAMAS

"Anatomy of a Shark Bite"

It might sound dumb to throw bloody chum into the waters of Walker's Cay, where dangerous bull sharks congregate, and then wade among the sharks in a Speedo while they're in the midst of a feeding frenzy. But not to "Unbiteable Erich" of Switzerland, a reputed expert in the body language of sharks.

The scientist believed that sharks can sense fear, and that his mastery of his heartbeat through yoga techniques made sharks regard him as a fellow predator, not fearful prey. Other shark experts advocate dressing in a black wetsuit, hood, and gloves to cover skin that resembles pale-colored prey in murky waters, but not Erich. He had "waded with sharks" for years. And this Wednesday, a video crew was prepared to tape him throwing fish into the water to attract bull sharks, then wading into the sea with bare legs to observe their body language.

The sharks are often accompanied by remora, quasi-parasite fish that clean the sharks and sometimes attach to them with a suction cup for long rides. Just after one remora swam between Erich's legs a shark followed, and—unaware that Erich's yoga techniques had turned him into a fellow predator—snapped off a huge chunk of his left calf. He was pulled from the water in shock and flown by air ambulance to West Palm Beach, Florida, where doctors tried to save the remains of his leg and his life.

He spent six weeks in the hospital trying to figure out what went wrong. He concluded that nothing went wrong; *the shark simply mistook his leg for the remora in the murky water.*

The documentary, originally intended to prove Erich's theory that bull sharks will not attack unless provoked, was retitled *Anatomy of a Shark Bite.* A former colleague told a diving magazine: "It was an accident waiting to happen. He's more like a philosopher than a scientist. There's no evidence to support his theories."

Erich is no longer called "Unbiteable."

Reference: *Western Daily Press, The Telegraph,* Cyber Divers Network News

Hundreds of shark species have been identified, but just three species are responsible for most attacks on humans: the great white (<u>Carcharodon carcharias</u>), tiger (<u>Galeocerdo cuvier</u>), and bull shark (<u>Carcharhinus leucas</u>). Divers often encounter bull sharks. Their preference for shallow coastal waters makes them potentially the most dangerous sharks of all.

More information:

www.DarwinAwards.com/book/shark.html

PERSONAL ACCOUNT: *BUFO MARINUS*
1985, AUSTRALIA

During my undergraduate years at James Cook University, I read a short article in the local newspaper regarding the peculiar antics of a pair of biology students required to dissect a cane toad.

The South American cane toad, *Bufo marinus*, was introduced to Australia as a biological control for the cane beetle, which destroys millions of dollars of sugar cane each year. This was an environmental disaster! First, the toad never developed a taste for cane beetles, but instead slaked its prodigious appetite with all manner of endemic fauna. Second, its toxins are not restricted solely to the two poison sacs behind its head, making it poisonous fare for Australian wildlife during every stage of its lifecycle.

In short, this toad eats anything smaller than it is, and poisons anything bigger.

Back in the laboratory, one student confidently bet his lab partner $20 that he would not swallow the ovaries of the cane toad they were dissecting. In need of money, and impressed with the magnanimous offer, the lab partner ate the organs. He suffered FOUR cardiac arrests while in transit to the hospital.

He is not eligible for a Darwin Award, since he did not die, but I suggest that he deserves an Honorable Mention.

The final sentence in the article suggested that we still do not know enough about the cocktail of toxins possessed by the cane toad.

Reference: *Townsville Bulletin*

Toads of the genus <u>Bufo</u> secrete a poison-ous, mildly hallucinogenic alkaloid called bufotenin, $C_{12}H_{16}N_2O$. For pictures of cane toads, visit:

www.DarwinAwards.com/book/bufo.html

I want to hear from a reader from Townsville who can wade through the back issues and check the details.

PERSONAL ACCOUNT:
DODGING THE DRAFT HORSE
SPRING 1942, WISCONSIN

My late great-grandfather told me this story, and my great-uncle swears it really happened. During World War II, Larry Shaw, a nineteen-year-old college dropout, received notice he was to be drafted. He was given orders to report to an army recruiting post. Already having lost an uncle and a cousin to the Japanese, Larry was afraid to go. He was aware that if he wasn't in perfect health, the army would reject him. But if he hurt himself on purpose, he would go to jail!

Larry, who worked at a farm with my great-grandfather, came up with a plan to "accidentally" hurt himself just enough to avoid the war, in a manner believable enough to pass as an accident.

While he and his coworkers were in the field, and without alerting any of them to his intentions, Larry walked up to a horse and tried to get it to step on his foot and break his toes. The horse, however, refused to move. No matter how much Larry pushed and shoved the horse, he couldn't get it to step on him. After trying for a long time, the frustrated Darwin hopeful got mad and kicked the horse in the tail. The startled horse responded by kicking back.

Larry was struck in the throat and died a few hours later, successfully dodging the draft, if not the kick.

Reference: Personal Account

PERSONAL ACCOUNT:
WATCH WHERE YOU'RE GOING
SUMMER 2003, USA

I hired several laborers to prepare two garden areas for me. They needed some supplies, so I showed them the location of ice water and the bathroom, and left to obtain the supplies. Upon my return, I found an ambulance in front of my home, along with two police cars.

The police informed me that the neighbor had called 911 to report a naked man screaming and running around my yard.

As it turned out, one of the laborers had needed to answer the call of nature. Rather than use the bathroom, he went into the woods behind our house, dropped his trousers, and squatted down—right on top of a huge nest of hornets.

He was released from the hospital after a week, having learned a very painful and nearly fatal lesson: *Always watch where you're going.*

Reference: Cy Stapleton, Personal Account

PERSONAL ACCOUNT: SHORTCUT CUT SHORT
SUMMER 1990, CALGARY, CANADA

Although this story does not qualify for a Darwin, I'd like to share the most spectacular case of extreme stupidity I've ever seen. I was a soldier of the Lord Strathcona's Horse, an armored regiment stationed in Calgary. We were hosting elements of the British Army at Canada's main training center in Wainwright, Alberta. I think they were the 17th/21st Lancers.

We took some of our new British friends to town, to party at the Wainwright Hotel bar. Around one A.M., we decided to save cab money and walk back to the base. This was a trek of about three miles, because one must detour around a large, fenced pasture to reach the front gate.

That pasture holds some of the last Plains bison in Canada, a herd of about forty animals. Bison are not the friendliest ruminants on the planet. Safety signs are posted every ten feet along the fence, and warnings read, "Unless you can cross this pasture in nine seconds, do not attempt it. The bison can do it in ten."

We reached the pasture and started to walk around it, but one of our drunken Brit companions decided that the warnings were fake. "Real, live buffalo don't exist!" Despite our protests, he opted for a shortcut. He hopped over the five-foot fence and disappeared into the dark field.

We watched and waited.

Seconds later, a high-pitched and very un-British profanity was heard from the pasture, and our friend came tearing back toward the fence at a speed that would have done credit to Donovan Bailey, the fastest man in the world. A fully mature and quite unhappy Plains bison thundered behind him.

The only reason the young gunner survived was sheer, fear-induced acceleration. He vaulted the five-foot fence without breaking stride. His rear foot caught on the top rail, sending him spinning into the grass on the safe side, half a second before two thousand pounds of extremely unfriendly hamburger smashed into the fence at full steam.

The fence is constructed of extremely solid steel pipes, yet the two-foot dent made by the bison remains to this day. The animal staggered, snorted, shook his head, and rumbled off with a splitting headache. Our friend escaped with a broken ankle, moderate concussion, dislocated shoulder, and a great deal of bleeding from his uncontrolled landing.

Had he not cleared the fence, he would have been pile-driven to smithereens by the huge bull. Fear had drained the alcohol from our systems, but we were still laughing too hard to be sympathetic as we gave him first aid and summoned help.

If you're looking for the dent, it's on the "town" side of the paddock, about halfway up. Last I heard, it was still there.

Reference: David R. Organ, Personal Account; *Edmonton Journal*

Readers say bison aren't just strong, they're also quick. They have seen a buffalo cow toss a pesky calf twenty feet off to the side with perfect grace and absolutely no strain. In Yellowstone Park, they report many instances of bison overturning cars, trucks, and snowmobiles with men, women, and children on board. Bison are noted for their ability to stand off a full-grown grizzly bear.

READER COMMENT:

"I am wondering if rear feet only occur in Britain."

CHAPTER 5

Alcohol

Alcohol plays a role in many Darwin Awards, but this is the first chapter devoted exclusively to the bone-headed things we do while inebriated. Get ready for a spy device, freeway calisthenics, saliva, bar bets, sunglasses, revenge, a beer-filled condom, window glass, a drinking glass, auto repair, firecrackers, and a submarine. But before you settle in with that glass of wine, read this science essay on the flu virus, and what it says about human evolution.

DISCUSSION: ENDOGENOUS RETROVIRUSES AND EVOLUTION

"More than a hypothesis, it's a theory!"

Stephen Darksyde, Science Writer

Every winter as the season turns and Santa comes to visit, a less welcomed traveler makes the rounds. It's influenza, a truly horrid little critter. And right now, in the throes of delirium, flush with fever and cold, I confess; I really despise influenza. I go to sleep feeling chipper and wake up feeling beaten with baseball bats and heated by a microwave to a toasty 103 degrees.

This damn flu is caused by a virus, of course, just one of many viral pathogens that curse mankind. No one knows how these quasi-living, self-replicating packets of genetic material first came to be. Perhaps they're a vestigial remnant of a long-gone RNA-based world that thrived in the nearly boiling sea of a planet unrecognizable as Earth, billions of years ago. Maybe they're errant bits of code from a more traditional bacterial microbe that began freelancing on its own.

However they arose, the viral vector is here to stay.

They all have the same grisly modus operandi. First, the dastardly buggers break through the cell wall. Some pick the lock of an existing portal and sneak past the molecular door-man disguised as legitimate cargo. Others are constructed like an off-shore drilling platform. They land on jointed legs, drop a drill bit onto the exterior of their target, and then begin boring in for all they're worth.

Once the membrane is breached by whatever means, viruses inject a packet of trouble into the interior, which makes for the nucleus and commandeers the genetic machinery to make more viruses. The end result is a person who sickens, and sometimes dies.

But there is a consolation prize. Geneticists have found that this viral scourge is incredibly useful in shedding light on all manner of mysteries biological.

Viruses Are Our Friends, Part 1

Some of these little influenza bugs are *retroviruses* like HIV and feline leukemia.

> **retrovirus (n):** genes carried on single-stranded RNA, which co-opts the nucleus of the infected cell to convert itself into DNA. This DNA sometimes inserts itself into the cell's chromosomal DNA.

These viruses are RNA, and typically "reverse-transcribe" their RNA into DNA for integration into the host's genome. When that happens, they snip the DNA and insert themselves surreptitiously into the host's chromosome, where they lie

dormant, sometimes for years, before activating. Later, they activate and begin making more RNA, which in turn inserts *itself* into the genome, until the entire cell basically falls apart. Then the RNA retroviruses are off to seek new, healthy cells for more viral adventures.

But if the retrovirus doesn't reactivate, this life cycle fails. While the infection is contained, the cell is left with inert viral sequences scattered throughout its genome. They can cause problems. The inert sequences may disrupt a key gene, for example, and uncontrolled replication may ensue—the beginning of cancer. Or it could spark an autoimmune disorder like multiple sclerosis, or exotic forms of painful, debilitating inflammatory disease. But often the retrovirus simply sits in the chromosome, inert and disregarded.

Now consider inheritance. Sometimes, by a stroke of fate, the infected host is a sperm or egg cell, which becomes a child. That child has those inert viral sequences in every single cell of his body. If those sequences happen to lie near an allele (one member of a pair of genes) that becomes ubiquitous in the population through natural selection, then all members of the species will carry the same genetic "signature" in every cell of their body. These ghosts of infections past are called *endogenous retroviruses*, or more affectionately, ERVs.

An ERV found in the same DNA location in two people provides powerful evidence, admissible in court, that they share a common ancestor. All humans share many ERVs in identical locations, which is no surprise. We all have common ancestors if one looks far enough back. But here's where it gets interesting: Chimps and humans also have ERVs in common. If identical ERVs serve as evidence of relatedness in court, then

ERVs are equally convincing evidence that chimps and humans are related!

The human and chimp genomes have been sequenced over the last decade, and we've found a dozen separate ERVs (hundreds of repeats each) identical in both genomes, in exactly the same locations. When these sequences are checked for time of introduction, they indicate a common ancestor five to seven million years ago. That is consistent with other molecular divergence studies and the fossil record.

But wait, there's more!

Consider a repeat sequence of base pairs like an ERV—or any other nonfunctional DNA sequence for that matter—found in the same locations in the genome between two species. Geneticists have looked at shared sequences between humans and mice, and compared those to the shared sequences between humans and chimps. They found that in humans and chimps, the same mouse sequences have been overwritten, just like a new CD recorded over an old one. This is exactly what we'd expect if ancestors of chimps and humans diverged more recently than primates and rodents diverged.

Creationists hate ERVs. They usually ignore them, or recursively label them "intelligent common design." ERVs have no known function. They code for viral proteins used only by viruses. Even if these things did have a function to us, common descent (common ancestors) explains how they got where they are in both species. The odds against two species by sheer chance being identically infected are enormous: one in ten followed by a hundred zeros. You have a better chance of winning the lottery ten times in a row than of being infected

by a dozen distinct ERVs in the same hundreds of locations in your genome as any other individual or creature.

Viruses Are Our Friends, Part 2

Viruses do more than shed light on evolutionary relationships. Their study holds great promise for novel health therapies. We may someday tailor viruses that eat only cancer cells. And since a virus can literally perform nano-surgery on the chromosomes of a cell without so much as breaking the patient's skin, we might enlist them to remove genetic abnormalities and replace the pathological sequences with healthy ones. Inherited susceptibility toward cardiopulmonary disease, diabetes, and cancer—the three greatest killers of humanity—might be permanently eliminated. Afflictions like sickle-cell anemia, lupus, irritable bowel syndrome, muscular dystrophy, Lou Gehrig's disease, and on and on, would all become words found only in history books. What a wonderful gift of health to bestow on our children!

Science is slowly but surely domesticating the virus. This is only fair. We've suffered from these little beasts for way too long. A little payback is overdue. At least that's my firm opinion as I lie here immobilized with flu on the couch, temporarily lucid between waves of total mental incapacitation. God, my body aches . . . *Where the hell did I put that aspirin?*

Now that it has been firmly established that mankind evolved from mice and monkeys, here are stories of inebriated innovations that make mice and monkeys cringe when we say we're related to them. . . .

DARWIN AWARD: HOMEMADE WINE
UNCONFIRMED BY DARWIN
2004, GEORGIA

At a "convenience dump," where local residents could drop off waste for later delivery to the main county dump, monitors were paid to ensure that residents deposited only allowed waste. One keen-eyed inspector noticed a bottle in the trash compactor that looked suspiciously like homemade wine. He fished the bottle out of the compactor. At this point, you may be thinking this is a "man crushed by compactor" story—but no!

After safely retrieving the bottle, the gentleman in question and another local man proceeded to drink the "wine." Apparently, neither of them took a clue from the fact that the bottle had been thrown away in a dump, leading to the reasonable conclusion that its contents were undrinkable. This particular vintage was antifreeze. Both men were poisoned, and one died.

Ironically, if the men had actually been drinking wine along with their antifreeze, both might have lived. Ethanol is sometimes used in hospitals to counteract the deadly effects of antifreeze poisoning. Antifreeze is not toxic until the ethylene glycol is converted to oxalic acid, which crystallizes and damages the kidneys. Since the *alcohol dehydrogenase* enzyme is the first step in forming oxalic acid, the reaction is inhibited by administering a dose of ethanol, which competes for the enzyme.

Reference: Radio news report

More about ethanol as a competitive inhibitor:

www.DarwinAwards.html/book/inhibitor.html

DARWIN AWARD: FREEWAY DANGLER
Confirmed by Darwin
31 MAY 2005, SEATTLE, WASHINGTON

Strength and endurance are two of the most important characteristics that can be passed on to improve the species, so physical challenges between males are frequent. In this case, two drinking buddies found themselves on an overpass forty feet above a busy freeway in downtown Seattle at 2:45 A.M. It turned out to be the perfect place to determine who had more strength and endurance. Whoever could dangle from the overpass the longest would win!

Unfortunately, the winner was too tired from his victory to climb back up, despite help from his thirty-one-year-old friend. The unidentified champion fell smack into the front of a semi barreling down the highway at sixty miles per hour and bounced onto the pavement, where he was hit by a car. The car did not stop. Authorities did not identify the winner of the competition.

Reference: KIRO-TV, *Seattle Times*, *Seattle Post-Intelligencer*, AP

DARWIN AWARD: SPY VS. SELF

Confirmed by Darwin

28 MAY 2004, CURSI, ITALY

"Hold my beer and watch this!"

Fabio, twenty-eight, left the family ostrich business for a new career as a truck driver. But his interests were more eclectic than the average ostrich-farming truck driver. Relaxing one evening with friends at a pub, Fabio shifted the conversation to his new interest in spy gadgets. He pulled an ordinary-looking pen out of his pocket and explained that it was actually a single-shot pistol. To demonstrate, he pointed it at his head and clicked the button. The cleverly disguised gadget worked perfectly, sending a fatefully fatal .22-caliber bullet into Fabio's left occipital lobe.

Reference: *La Repubblica, La Gazzetta del Mezzogiorno*

DARWIN AWARD: FAILED FRAME-UP

Confirmed by Darwin
19 MARCH 2005, MICHIGAN

"Unusual" and "complicated" is how the Missaukee County sheriff described the mysterious death of nineteen-year-old Christopher.

After an evening spent imbibing large quantities of alcohol, Christopher noticed a shortage in his liquor supply that could not be attributed to his own depredations. He concluded that his neighbor had stolen a bottle of booze! He menaced the neighbor with a knife, to no avail, whereupon he retired to his own apartment to brood about revenge.

Finally he figured out the perfect way to get back at that conniving bottle-thief: Christopher would stab himself and blame the neighbor!

A witness saw Christopher enter the bathroom as he called 911. He calmly informed the dispatcher that his neighbor had stabbed him. Witnesses said he looked fine when he emerged from the bathroom, but a moment later gouts of blood spewed from his chest. Suddenly he began screaming, begging for help. The dispatcher heard a woman shout, "Why did you do this?" He collapsed at the door of his apartment.

Deputies arrived quickly, but Christopher had already bled to death from self-inflicted stab wounds to his chest. An autopsy determined that he had stabbed himself twice.

The first wound apparently didn't look dangerous enough, so he tried again. The second time, the knife plunged into his left ventricle. This wound was plenty dangerous: He had only two minutes to live.

Christopher died in vain. His deathbed accusation of his neighbor failed, as a witness confirmed that the neighbor was not in the apartment. All Christopher got for revenge was an accidental death sentence.

Reference: *Cadillac News*

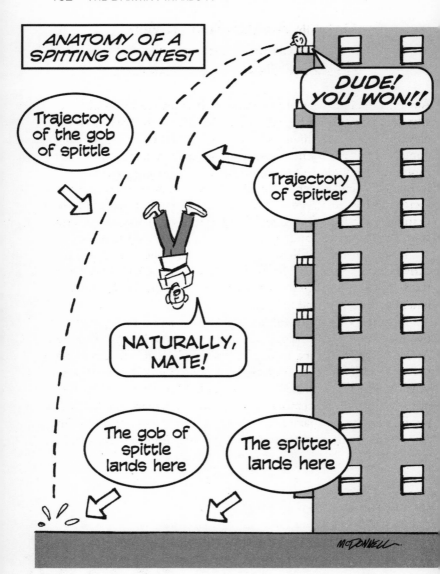

Darwin Award: Aim to Win
Confirmed by Darwin
21 February 2004, Ottawa, Canada

Ameer, a second-year engineering student at Carleton University, was celebrating his twentieth birthday with friends in his eleventh-floor apartment when they embarked on a spitting contest. His two friends had already made their marks. Ameer thought he could use his engineering skills to improve his performance. A quick mental calculation of trajectory, projectile velocity, and wind speed indicated that winning required more than a simple "stand and spit" technique. Ameer took a running start, flew over the balcony railing, and plunged to his death.

"It was purely accidental," said Ottawa police. "Momentum carried him beyond." The building's security guard heard the thud. "He was one of the smartest guys I ever met in my life. He had a maturity beyond his age."

Spitting contest deaths are becoming a trend. In 1999, a twenty-five-year-old soldier in Alabama won the first Darwin Award in this category, using the same technique and achieving the same result from a three-story vantage point. Twenty-three-year-old Bartosz of Illinois was nominated for falling twenty feet onto his head in December 2005. Bartosz is remarkable for having fallen over an apartment railing without a running start. But Ameer clearly trumps his competitors with his eleven-story fall.

Perhaps the three have reunited in the afterlife, arm in arm, sailing through the air, their projectiles suspended in front of them like bullets in the *Matrix* movies.

Reference: *Ottawa Sun, La Presse*

Darwin Award: Damned if You Do . . .

Confirmed by Darwin

6 September 2004, Romania

A Pitesti man with a metal ring stuck on his penis was being sought by doctors, after he fled the hospital consumed by panic.

The unidentified forty-two-year-old said he put the ring on his penis after losing a bet during a drinking game at a pub. He was subsequently unable to remove the ring. Embarrassment kept him from seeking immediate medical help, but after two days, unbearable pain overcame unbearable shame, and he took his smelly and discolored member in for treatment.

Doctors told him the bad news. Gangrene had set in, and his life was in danger. The blood supply had been cut off for too long, and there was nothing they could do but remove his penis, so that the necrosis did not spread to the rest of his body.

The manhunt was ongoing. "There is no way he can escape going under the knife," said a doctor. "He must come back to the hospital and accept this." The man's only consolation is a guaranteed Darwin Award, one way or the other!

Reference: *Daily Record* (U.K.), Ananova

A reader says, "NOT TRUE! Some of us naturally 'little guys' have managed to have a kid or two, with a little creativity and medical intervention. Surgically cutting a tendon over the penis gives an extra inch or more."

DARWIN AWARD: KILLER SHADES

Confirmed by Darwin

17 SEPTEMBER 2003, SAN FRANCISCO, CALIFORNIA

Barry Bonds had just made the last out at the bottom of the eighth. At that very moment, Todd had bummed one last beer from a new friend at the San Francisco Giants' ballpark.

Todd was leaning on the railing of the Arcade port walk, getting to the "bottom eighth" of his beer, when his Maui Jim* designer sunglasses slipped off the top of his head. Down they fell, landing twenty-five feet below, where a helpful bum picked them up and tried to toss them back. But it was too far! Todd called out that he was coming down to get them.

Todd had recently relocated to Santa Cruz for the gnarly waves at Mavericks. His wife described him as "a passionate surfer" talented enough to turn pro. Perhaps his sense of physical prowess was his downfall. The agile thirty-eight-year-old considered and rejected the long walk down, in favor of a quicker alternative. He would climb over the railing, jump to a perch on a light sconce five feet below, then drop like Tarzan to the ground, gratefully reclaiming his shades from the bum.

At least, that was the plan. And the first part, climbing the railing, went fine. The second part was more problematic. Todd missed the sconce and "came down like a pancake," according to a startled observer a few feet from the point of impact. The crowd was shocked into silence. Why would anyone risk his life for a pair of shades?

*Maui Jim sunglasses retail for as much as $200.

Todd would have been chagrined to hear the observer's next words. "They looked cheap," he said, apologizing, "I don't know sunglass brands."

Reference: *San Francisco Examiner, San Jose Mercury News, Santa Cruz Sentinal*

HONORABLE MENTION:
A MEDICAL FIRST AT OKTOBERFEST
Confirmed by Darwin
SEPTEMBER 2002, MUNICH, GERMANY

Three doctors published the following account in a highly respected medical journal. The man in question disqualified himself from a true Darwin Award by being smart enough to go to a hospital and admit what he'd done. The report is quoted directly from the journal, with the addition of bracketed "translations" that clarify the medical jargon.

"A thirty-one-year-old man was admitted to the emergency unit with severe abdominal pain and vomiting for two hours. [He'd been sober enough to notice a problem for the last two hours.] An abdominal radiograph disclosed an intestinal obstruction, and a small bowel follow-through study revealed a filling defect in the right-side jejunum. [His gut was backed up because something was stuck in it.] Persistent exploration of the patient's history [he *really* didn't want to talk about it] disclosed a visit to the Munich Oktoberfest the night before, during which the patient had ingested a condom filled with beer. [No, we don't know why, either.]

"Upper endoscopy was unsuccessful in removing the condom. [We couldn't budge it.] Because the condom was localized close to the abdominal wall, it was finally punctated with a long needle under CT control. [We stuck a really big needle in it, and it burst.] Forty milliliters of a yellow clear liquid [we can't say in print that it was beer, because we were laughing so hard we didn't think to send it to the lab] were drawn off when the condom slid

forward spontaneously. The next morning, the condom was identified in the patient's stool [a high-quality, leakage-resistant condom, showing that the man was at least attempting to nullify his influence on the gene pool], and the patient was discharged in good condition."

The authors note, "To the best of our knowledge, this is the first report on intestinal obstruction caused by ingestion of a condom filled with an alcoholic beverage, and its successful transcutaneous treatment. [Hey, we always wanted to be the first doctors to do *something*!]"

Reference: *American Journal of Gastroenterology*, February 2003; 98:512, with "translations" by T. G. Shaw

Because dissolved CO_2 outgasses when a beer warms, a condom of cool beer swells after ingestion, and can stop up the plumbing. The swallower may have assumed he was beating a Breathalyzer by delivering the alcohol straight to his stomach. But that won't work, because the Breathalyzer tests for alcohol that comes from blood gases that exude from the lungs.

PERSONAL ACCOUNT: POWER OVER PLATE GLASS
2001, GUILDFORD, ENGLAND

During a short spell as a police constable, I came to be involved in a reported "serious incident." Police were called in to assist a severely injured lad of sixteen who was being rushed to the hospital with a nearly severed foot. The victim said he had been walking away from a nightclub when he and a friend became embroiled in an altercation with an unknown person or persons, resulting in his being thrown through a ten-foot plate-glass shop window. The area was sealed off, large amounts of blood on the footpath photographed and washed away for sanitary reasons, and the owner of the windowless store notified.

On reaching the hospital and sobering up, the victim explained the true story. The somewhat intoxicated young buck had bet his friend that he could smash the shop window. After all, he was a fit footballer with powerful legs. And did I say drunk? To make his point, he stood with his back to the glass and performed a "donkey kick" into the bottom of the window.

Our lad failed to take the following points into consideration: Glass is easier to break if you hit the edge, as the energy can dissipate effectively. And the plate glass in this case was 1.5 centimeters thick. Ten feet of thick plate glass falling straight down weighs a great deal.

Although he lost a lot of blood, the victim did not "kick the bucket" and hence this is only an Honorable Mention, but he did ruin any chance of a football career (though he kept his foot), and given the sexual antics of soccer stars he probably reduced the potential spread of his seed as a result.

I felt so sorry for him that I convinced my boss to authorize a police caution, even though the damage ran to more than £5000!

Heeoor, heeoor, heeoor to have known better!

Reference: Marc Buckingham, Personal Account; Surrey Police

PERSONAL ACCOUNT:
THE MAN WITH THE IRON STOMACH
2002, BELGIUM

One night, I partied all night at a discotheque with friends. Afterward, we went to a "bar of the king" that was open day and night. Such bars are known for housing thugs and pirates.

We, two men and two women, were sitting at a table drinking vodka and beer when a big, mean-looking man approached the table and started talking shit. He was so intoxicated that the collection of syllables he pronounced could hardly be classified as a language. The girls were annoyed by his presence and—typically—tried to get rid of him by calling him names.

In response, the man seized an empty beer glass (in Belgium, a beer glass is as thick as a normal jar) and bit into it, breaking off a piece. This behavior is common in men who have unresolved frustration and need to show their courage, so we weren't impressed. But then the man started chewing the glass, and quickly bit off another chunk, chewing and biting until only the very bottom of the glass remained, which he put back on the table.

We stared at the man as he chewed the pieces, and then heard the glass cracking. Some blood came out of his mouth. He then tried to swallow the glass, choked, and spat blood-soaked pieces onto the table. Then he started gargling blood and fell to his knees.

We were too paralyzed by the event to move, but the bartender ran up to help the man. He tried to remove the remaining glass from the man's mouth, but the man bit the bartender's finger. I called an ambulance from my cell phone. I don't know if the man survived. And I really don't know why he did it. But remember this: If you have an iron stomach, make sure that your throat is iron, too.

Reference: Personal Account

READER COMMENT:

"I think he had one jar too many."

PERSONAL ACCOUNT: VOLUNTEER FIREMAN
CA. 1978, INDIANA

My friend's father, Bob, was a volunteer fireman and a home mechanic. He was also a heavy drinker who never seemed to be without booze in his hand. One day I was helping him repair one of their cars. Bob, already well into a six-pack when I arrived, believed that the fuel line was blocked. His solution began with jacking the car up a few feet and draining the twelve gallons of gasoline from the tank.

In the process of disconnecting the fuel line from the tank, gasoline spilled all over Bob, soaking his polyester shirt and flooding the floor of the garage. Bob then used several five-gallon buckets to catch the remaining gasoline that was pouring out of the tank. Although the garage door was open to allow ventilation, the fumes were so thick that my friend and I had to step outside to breathe. Bob continued to lie on the garage floor, in a pool of gasoline under the car.

> The universal building code requires gas-fired hot-water tanks in garages to be at least eighteen inches off the floor, to prevent accidental combustion of gasoline fumes. Since gasoline fumes are heavy and stay near the floor, eighteen inches is considered a safe height. And it would be, under normal circumstances. But the circumstances in this case were not normal.

At about that time, the water heater, located about ten feet from gasoline-soaked Bob, kicked on. The entire floor went up in flames, and a large fireball came out the garage door toward us. My friend and I dove to the ground to avoid the flames.

After the initial blast, Bob picked himself up and—reacting as the trained and experienced firefighter he was—grabbed a fire extinguisher and put out the flames. Only then did he realize that his polyester shirt had melted to his now thoroughly burned chest. He refused his wife's assistance and, despite his inebriated state, drove himself to the local hospital.

Bob lost most of the skin on his chest and most of the hair on his head. He also spent several days in the burn unit, and was ultimately tossed out of the local volunteer fire department.

Reference: George Leavell, Personal Account

PERSONAL ACCOUNT: BULLET-BRAIN
CA. 1950S, SOMEWHERE UNDER THE SEA

My grandfather served for ages in the Royal Navy, and he related this story to me about his time aboard a rivet-hulled diesel-electric submarine. Two men, the ship's petty officer and an ordinary seaman, were drinking in the mess wardroom. Having cheerfully consumed all the available alcohol (presumably above and beyond the daily ration of rum), the seaman asked the petty officer to do him a favor. He wanted a bullet shot through his hat.

Because a breach in the hull could be deadly to the entire crew, and because a ricocheting bullet would be dangerous to the crew in such close quarters even if it did not puncture the hull, firearms are locked up aboard ship. Nevertheless, the petty officer honored his friend's request, retrieved a 9 mm Beretta from his locker, and in an alcoholic haze opened fire on the hat, which was still on his friend's head.

> At depth, a submarine hull is under pressure, but the atmosphere inside is not. That's why the crew doesn't suffer from the "bends" as the submarine submerges and surfaces. This pressure difference makes a breach in the hull very dangerous. If the hull is under ten atmospheres of pressure (at one hundred meters) a breach could fill 90 percent of the interior with water.

Despite the amount of alcohol consumed, he was pretty much bang on target. Ignoring the ricocheting bullet and the screams as the rest of the crew ducked, the ordinary seaman removed his hat and examined the bullet hole that had pierced it just an inch from his head. "Too far away," he said. "I want it closer in. Have another shot." Famous last words. The next bullet creased him along his skull, and hurled him to the floor, bleeding and unconscious.

Both men were tossed out of the Royal Navy.

My grandfather recently told this story to his table during one of those seamen's dinner-and-dance parties, and was shocked when one man eyed him coldly and informed him that it had been his uncle on the receiving end of the bullet!

Reference: Joshua Sinyor, Personal Account

PERSONAL ACCOUNT: BLACKCATS IN THE PANTS
FOURTH OF JULY, SOMEWHERE IN AMERICA

Some say persistence is a virtue, and in science that is often the case. Great scientists frequently push the edge in their experiments, extending their hypothesis as they prove each successive point. When tests are performed with firecrackers, though, there is the chance that going to extremes can lead to an amateur scientist's untimely removal from the gene pool.

Two young men, "Einstein" and "Teller," were at a friend's house celebrating Independence Day with a little food, a little booze, and many fireworks. Einstein was startled to discover a pack of firecrackers exploding at his feet and looked up to see Teller laughing, lighter still in hand. Einstein yelled, "You're stupid to throw explosives so close to a human being!"

"Firecrackers can't hurt you," said Teller, and to prove his point, he unwrapped another pack, lit its fuse, and dropped it at his own feet. As the firecrackers were popping, he said, "See, no damage!"

They argued and drank and argued and drank. Teller was convinced that his hypothesis was correct: Firecrackers could not hurt people. Einstein remained skeptical. Finally, Teller lit another pack, pulled the elastic band of his boxers forward, and dropped the pack down his underpants.

Before the firecrackers even started exploding, Teller began screaming as the fuse burned his skin. As they began to blow up, he screamed even louder and ran into the house.

Teller took himself to the hospital, and returned with burn ointment and the instruction to lay off work for a week. He refused to reveal the exact results of his experiment to Einstein, except to say that "both the twigs and berries" had been burned. The doctor warned him that his ability to reproduce was thereafter in question.

Reference: Personal Account

CHAPTER 6

Explosion/Fire

Pyrotechnics aren't just for professionals; amateurs frequently find the allure of explosives too great to pass up. With grenades, bombs, dynamite, gasoline, a mine detonator, electricity, ammunition, acetylene, chemicals, methane, lots of fireworks, a fire-breather, a bungee cord, and even a lava lamp, there's never a shortage of examples for fire-safety courses! This chapter begins with a science essay on the biggest explosion in the history of the planet. . . .

DISCUSSION:
CHICKEN LITTLE WAS RIGHT

Norm Sleep, Science Writer

Darwin Awards are minor personal catastrophes compared to a recent global catastrophe suffered by the Earth itself. If we don't protect ourselves from a repeat, the human race will earn an inevitable mass Darwin Award.

Yucatan, early June, sixty-five million years ago

The summer day begins as usual on the shallow reef. Fish and ammonites forage among the vegetation as they try to avoid becoming shark bait. Pterodactyls soar in the trade winds, waiting for tidbits. Suddenly, the sky to the south brightens like a second sunrise. Within seconds, the entire sky glows at white heat. Every mobile organism instinctively dives for cover. But there is no hope for them. One second later, coming in fast and at a low angle, an asteroid fifteen kilometers in diameter crashes to earth at twenty kilometers per second, vaporizing itself and the upper few kilometers of its center of impact. The shock produces a crater as wide as the Mediterranean Sea. A thick blanket of hot rock fragments fries every living thing within a few hundred kilometers of the crater rim.

How do we know when this impact took place? We know the time of year from clues frozen in ponds and preserved in the geological record. The time of day is artistic license, because more goes on during the day than at night.

The pent-up rock vapor expands, carried rapidly northward by the momentum of the projectile. Within minutes, the vapor cloud sears the surface of western North America, igniting any exposed plant or animal. This is not an ordinary forest fire; the massive heat wave destroys even seeds buried underground.

Several minutes later, across the ocean in Europe and Australia, dawn comes early as ejected sand-sized fragments return to Earth at cosmic velocities. They glow like meteors, filling the sky for hours. Their heat ignites exposed vegetation, leaving surviving animals with nothing to eat. Soot from the fires fills the lower atmosphere, quickly bringing darkness.

The calamity is just beginning. The meteor fragments vaporize into a fine dust that circulates in the upper atmosphere, blotting out sunlight. Sulfate, vaporized from anhydrite beds beneath the Yucatan, contributes to the opaqueness of the stratosphere. It remains in the air longer than the dust. Darkness brings cold after the heat. Lilies freeze in Wyoming ponds. Photosynthesis stops in the open ocean for more than a year. Plankton species perish, along with the creatures in the

food chain above them. Animals not dependent on photosyn-thesis eke out a living. Survivors include crocodiles in ponds, our insect-eating ancestors in logs, and a species of shore bird—the only remaining dinosaur.

Long before the great asteroid forever changed life on Earth, even worse disasters occurred that make this more re-cent apocalypse pale, a mere pebble in a pond. Four billion years ago, objects *hundreds* of kilometers in diameter hurtled from the sky, reshaping the planets. These gigantic impacts produced the enormous basins still visible on the Moon and Mars. The heat from the kinetic energy of the projectiles partly vaporized the whole terrestrial ocean. Amazingly, life was able to weather these storms in the "Goldilocks Zone," which is located in rocks over a kilometer deep, the only safe place for thousands of years after an impact. The surface and shallow subsurface alternately teemed with life, and became a death trap when a large asteroid hit every few ten million years. Both the surface and the deep subsurface were too hot to sustain life. Only heat-loving (thermophilic) organisms in the Goldilocks Zone, living at 100 degrees Centigrade, sur-vived these tribulations to root the tree of life.

Evolution does not directly prepare organisms for condi-tions they do not regularly experience, like a year of darkness in the tropical ocean. So most organisms are unable to cope with the disastrous results of such freak events. Some adapta-tions that arose to cope with other environmental conditions, however, provided salvation for a species. For example, in pre-human times the pike evolved sharp teeth for catching and eat-ing its usual diet of smaller fish. Today, these teeth are advantageous for biting through fishing line. Other coinciden-tal adaptations help during rare events. For example, sixty-five million years ago, when most creatures boiled to death during the great cataclysm, animals and plants that were low on the food chain and nestled deep in swamps managed to survive.

Chicken Little was right—the risk is real!

Your chance of being killed by an asteroid is about the same as in a passenger plane crash: one in a million per year. But with an asteroid, billions of humans will be killed at the same time. How do we avoid the indignity of a mass extinction, with no one left to bury us? Our species possesses one helpful adaptation: our intelligence, which has evolved for hunting, gathering, and social interaction. Unlike dinosaurs, we can observe, predict, and act decisively. Can our smarts save us from an otherwise inevitable tragedy?

Asteroid orbits are predictable in the short run, but over a geological length of time the orbits change. The Earth is a tiny target in the vastness of the solar system. Moreover, earth-crossing orbits are chaotic—a series of minute changes in an asteroid's actual position and velocity build up to huge changes over time. Thus, in the long term, asteroid orbits are effectively random—more so than even a fair roulette table. We know an asteroid will hit us, sooner or later, but we can't say which one, or when.

Even a fair roulette wheel gives nonrandom results due to mechanical variations. By collecting statistics and betting appropriately, Joseph Jaggers broke the bank at Monte Carlo in 1873, and mathematician Claude Shannon built a wearable computer to outwit the roulette wheel in 1961. Nowadays, casinos regularly rebalance their wheels to keep the spin results as random as possible.

NASA monitors near-Earth asteroids. Before this program began a few years ago, we did not know whether an impact was more likely next year or a million years from now. Now, visual tracking and heavy mathematics predict the orbits of large objects five hundred years in the future. Early results are in: no ten-kilometer-diameter object has Earth's name on it. And five centuries from now, society should be better equipped to deal with the hazard of an impending collision. However, the more numerous one-kilometer objects also present a danger of global catastrophe. We do not yet have a complete manifest of these vermin of the sky.

What do we do if we find an asteroid in our path? Civilization will face this calamity sooner or later, certainly within a million years. If we have been diligent, we will have hundreds of years to prepare for an impact. We will be able to soft-land a probe to track the object's course and confirm the danger of collision. We will probably not choose to blow it up, as that would turn one dangerous object into several. More likely we will change its orbit by detonating a nuclear explosive nearby, to spall off some material. Newton's law of the conservation of energy predicts that the equal and opposite force would change the asteroid's orbital velocity by a few centimeters per second. At that time, there may even be advanced rocket motors with enough power to do the job.

The take-home message is that, thanks to the development of human intelligence and our continually increasing knowledge base, the next time an asteroid threatens to destroy the planet, there's a good chance that life on Earth will be saved. And even if most life is destroyed, take heart. After another sixty-five million years, the cycle of evolution may lead to another civilization with the ability to protect Earth against these behemoths from outer space.

With that cheerful note of impending doom, let's delve into those who avoid the problem of asteroid impacts by leaving the gene pool in their own explosive manner. . . .

DARWIN AWARD: CHIMNEY-CLEANING GRENADE

Confirmed by Darwin

13 JANUARY 2005, CROATIA

One fateful afternoon, fifty-five-year-old Marko retreated to his semidetached workshop to make himself a tool for chimney cleaning. The chimney was too high for a simple broom to work, but if he could attach a brush to a chain and then weigh it down with something, that would do the trick. But what could he use as a weight?

He happened to have the perfect object. It was heavy, yet compact. And best of all, it was made of metal, so he could weld it to the chain. He must have somehow overlooked the fact that it was also a hand grenade and was filled with explosive material.

Marko turned on his welding apparatus and began to create an arc between the chain and the grenade. When the metal heated up, the grenade exploded. The force of the explosion killed poor Marko instantly, blasting shrapnel through the walls of the shed and shattering the windshield of a Mercedes parked outside. Marko's sooty chimney was untouched, however.

Reference: *Vecernji List*

READER COMMENTS:

"This fellow made an 'ash' of himself."

"A cautionary tale for Santa."

"Soot-black humour."

"Sounds like he blew it!"

DARWIN AWARD: UNSAFE AND INSANE

Confirmed by Darwin

2003, AUSTRALIA

Parents often warn that firecrackers can blow your hand off, but as a twenty-six-year-old Australian learned, they can also remove your gonads from the gene pool. An ambulance rushed to a neighborhood park after receiving reports that a man was hemorrhaging from his behind. The mercifully unidentified man had placed a lit firecracker between the cheeks of his buttocks, stumbled, and fell upon it.

"We do caution people against these acts," said the local police.

The emergency surgeon said the resulting wound looked like "a war injury." The explosion was forced upward, "blasted a great hole in the pelvis, ruptured the urethra, and injured muscles," rendering the man incontinent as well as sexually dysfunctional. He survived to tell the tale, making him eligible for the dubious honor of a Living Darwin Award.

Reference: *Illawarra Mercury*

DARWIN AWARD: DO-IT-YOURSELF LAND MINE

Confirmed by Darwin

27 MAY 2004, CHIAVENNA, ITALY

When Peraldo found sticks of old dynamite in an abandoned stable on the hill above his vineyard, he decided to bury the problem. Some might think that burying unstable dynamite would be . . . unwise. But not Peraldo, a sixty-seven-year-old retired entrepreneur, who had been an explosives expert in the army. He had also worked as a licensed *fuochino* in charge of explosives at construction sites prior to his retirement. He knew the ways of things that go boom.

This dynamite had been sitting around for some time, decaying and sweating highly unstable nitroglycerin. Peraldo carefully placed the high explosives in a hole thirty meters away from the stable and gently covered them with loose earth. Apparently the mound was a little too high to be aesthetically attractive, so Peraldo began patting it down with his hands. . . .

The massive blast rocked the entire town of Chiavenna. Police rushed to the vineyard to investigate. Peraldo was found torn to shreds but, miraculously, still alive and able to elucidate what had happened before he expired from internal injuries.

Reference: www.espressonline.it

Darwin Award: "Plug Me In"

Confirmed by Darwin

7 March 2005, Vietnam

Nguyen, twenty-one, was drinking with friends in Hanoi when he pulled out an old detonator he had found. It was about six centimeters long and eight centimeters in diameter, with two wires hanging out. Because it was old and rusty, Nguyen said, it couldn't explode. His friends disagreed.

To prove his point, Nguyen put the detonator in his mouth and the dangling wires were plugged into a 220-volt electrical receptacle.

Turns out Nguyen was wrong!

The victim had little time to reflect on his mistake, or whether 220 volts alone could have been fatal. According to police, "the explosion blew out his cheeks and smashed all his teeth." He died on the way to the hospital.

Reference: Deutsche Presse Agentur

Reader Comment:

"I guess he ate his words."

Darwin Award: Workin' at the Car Wash

Confirmed by Darwin

29 January 2003, Brazil

At work, Manoel was responsible for cleaning out the storage tanks of gasoline tanker trucks. He had been employed in that capacity for two months when he ran afoul of fuel.

The thirty-five-year-old began to fill a tanker with water, a standard safety procedure that forces flammable vapor out of the container. He returned an hour later to check whether the water level was high enough to proceed. But he had trouble deciding, because it was so DARK inside the tanker.

A resourceful employee, Manoel forgot the very reason he was filling the tank with water when he lit a cigarette lighter to shed some light on the situation. His little test successfully determined that the water level was not yet high enough for safety. The vapor explosion launched him through the air, and he landed in the company parking lot a hundred meters away.

Manoel suffered severe burns, blunt force trauma, and an injury to the head that exposed his unused brain, proving that he had one. Our witless car washer had learned his terminal lesson in safety by the time the firemen arrived.

Reference: *O Estado de São Paolo, Folha de São Paolo*

An aerospace engineering student comments, "I have a sound understanding of physics. This story says that the unfortunate victim flew one hundred meters, but people less than a mile from a nuclear bomb detonation rarely are thrown more than a hundred meters, and that's an explosion more than ten thousand times as powerful! I'm also a firefighter, and know that liquid fuel explosions don't have much mass and rarely throw a body far."

Darwin Award: Rocketing to Glory

Confirmed by Darwin

7 February 2005, Kuala Lumpur, Malaysia

Fireworks are a longstanding Lunar New Year's tradition among Malaysia's large Chinese minority, and they continue to be widely used to celebrate despite a ban on their sales and use.

Wan, a twenty-nine-year-old excavator operator, spent the evening watching people set off fireworks outside a suburban nightclub. These were no mere firecrackers. They were rockets that shot as high as a ten-story building before exploding.

His curiosity piqued, Wan bent over one of the launching tubes for a closer look, wondering how these powerful rockets worked. He was peering down the tube when it fired, sending him flying ten meters. He died instantly from severe head injuries, according to a senior police official.

Reference: *The Star*, AP

DARWIN AWARD: THE ARMY'S A BLAST

Confirmed by Darwin

6 MAY 2004, UKRAINE

Piling up live artillery is grueling work, so it makes perfect sense that a group of soldiers would take a cigarette break at lunchtime. The warehouse was filled with ninety-two thousand tons of ammunition—until the soldiers lit up their ciggies and inhaled deeply, ignoring warnings that smoking can cause cancer. They flicked the butts away and went back to work. The glowing embers of the tobacco butts acted like slow fuses, which started a small fire that nobody noticed until it ignited a chain reaction of massive explosions.

The explosions lasted for a week, tossing debris as far as twenty-five miles away, destroying buildings in a two-mile radius, and forcing the evacuation of thousands of nearby residents. Red-hot shrapnel set off additional fires in nearby towns and ruptured a minor gas pipeline. Total damage from the smoke break was estimated at $750 million.

Miraculously, only one of the soldiers at the arsenal died in the disaster.

Reference: Reuters, AP, Novosti

News accounts report five people killed by explosions, but only two were smokers. The nomination would be disqualified if innocent bystanders were injured—and an AP article said four died from "health problems aggravated by the stress of the disaster." Novosti, the Russian press agency, said six soldiers were charged with causing the fire, rather than two, and the only direct death was a guard at the facility. It's not clear if the guard was also smoking, or if the other four deaths were caused by the explosions or simply ill health. Therefore, I am tentatively calling this a Darwin Award, despite minor misgivings.

DARWIN AWARD: HUMAN TORCH

Confirmed by Darwin

23 NOVEMBER 2002, OSLO, NORWAY

Around 4:45 P.M., neighbors reported hearing a loud pop followed by a fire at a rail yard in Filipstad, just outside Oslo. Fearing a potential terrorist attack, fire and police crews rushed to the scene. The top of an electric train was burning! When the fire died down, investigators pieced together its cause.

The spray cans and wet paint on the side of the train were the first clues. Inner-city Norwegian youth, victims of a society polite to its core, were lashing out in desperation at the brutal cleanliness and order of a country where the trains always run on time, and they had decided to stick it to The Man by tagging the symbol of their oppression. So desperate were they to make their political point that they walked right past several signs warning of the danger of high voltage and climbed over fences to reach their objective.

One of them, a seventeen-year-old, wanted to tag where no man had tagged before—on the roof of the train. The fact that few people would ever see his art was no impediment to this brave young man as he sought to subvert the dominant paradigm. He climbed atop the train, sprayed his creation, and rose up to proclaim his accomplishment—touching the main power line and lighting up the neighborhood as fifteen thousand volts coursed through his body. His remains were so badly burned that authorities were initially unable to determine that the victim was human.

Reference: *Dagbladet, Aftenpost*

DARWIN AWARD: LAVA LAMP
Confirmed by Darwin
30 NOVEMBER 2004, WASHINGTON

Twenty-four-year-old Philip was found dead in the bedroom of his trailer home, with the burnt remains of a Lava Lamp strewn over his kitchen. Puzzled investigators eventually pieced together a likely scenario for Philip's last moments.

Lava Lamps are a mesmerizing distraction. Philip couldn't wait to fire up his new Lava Lamp. He plugged it in and waited for the pretty globs to begin their surreal dance. But after several frustrating minutes, nothing happened. Then a bright idea hit him: "Why not accelerate this painfully slow process?" He took the lamp to the kitchen, placed it on the stove, and turned up the heat.

In short order, the wax melted and began its sinuous dance. But the liquid was designed to be warmed by a forty-watt bulb, not gas flames. It was overheated. Entranced by the display, Philip forgot that "heat expands." Whereas there was no room for expansion in the glass bottle, the Lava Lamp resorted to a violent explosion to relieve the pressure.*

* Which is why the instructions warn NEVER to place the lamp directly on a heat source, such as a stove.

One thick shard of glass blew straight through Philip's chest and into his heart. Philip stumbled into his bedroom, perhaps uttering *"Aeternum vale!"* (Latin for "Farewell forever!") as he collapsed and died.

Police found no evidence of alcohol or drug use, so it is safely presumed that Philip was in full possession of his senses when he went out with a bang.

Reference: *Seattle Times, Seattle Post-Intelligencer*

The secret of the Lava Lamp is simple: A light bulb heats a bottle of colored wax and liquid. The wax is denser than the liquid at room temperature, and sits at the bottom. As the wax warms, it expands and rises in an undulating blob. At the top, where the bottle is cooler, the cooling wax becomes denser and begins to sink. The random, undulating effect is mesmerizing.

DARWIN AWARD: AMATEUR BOMB INSPECTOR
Confirmed by Darwin

25 MAY 2004, AMBON, INDONESIA

Curiosity may have killed this cat,
but no amount of satisfaction can bring him back.

The city of Ambon was on edge. Just two days before, a bomb hidden in a cookie tin, disguised with two bottles of beer and some peanuts, had exploded and wounded five people. So police took extra precautions when a worried man alerted them to a suspicious black plastic bag that had been hung on the handle of his motorbike while it was parked outside an open market.

The police cleared the area, moved the bag to the middle of the street, and waited for the bomb squad to arrive. Alarmingly, this bag also contained a cookie tin. The police set up a safety cordon twenty meters away from the bag and warned people to stay back. But after twenty-five minutes spent waiting for the bomb squad, curiosity got the best of Willem, a forty-five-year-old fish vendor, and a number of other onlookers. They wanted to get a closer look to see what else was in the bag. What could happen?

What, indeed. As they approached the bomb, it exploded, killing Willem and injuring sixteen others, all of whom receive Honorable Mentions.

Reference: *The Australian, Jakarta Post, Catholic World News, Taipei Times, Asia News, Christian Today*

HONORABLE MENTION: FIREWALLS
Confirmed by Darwin
1997, ENGLAND

There's ordinary foolishness, and then there's extraordinary foolishness. Stealing fireworks from a storage depot is foolishness. But using a welder's torch to cut through the wall of the building housing the fireworks—*that* is *extraordinary* foolishness.

Several burglars pushed their luck to the brink of failure when they tried to pull off a heist of a building containing a large volume of fireworks. They used a gas cutting torch to slice through the main door. The door was eight feet tall, concrete, and reinforced with a solid inch of steel. Just as the torch penetrated the door, and success was at hand . . . a spark landed in a crate of fireworks inside.

Fireworks are explosive, and this particular crate contained the equivalent of a hundred pounds of gunpowder. The entire factory exploded. The door was popped from its hinges and slammed flat into the ground. The roof lifted off and landed in one piece. Interestingly, despite the violence of the explosion, the debris was confined within the factory perimeter.

Astoundingly, the perpetrators were not killed, and have never been found. Their cutting equipment remained behind, along with their car, which had been flattened by the concrete roof. Flabbergasted pyrotechnics professionals have dubbed them the "Hole in the Ground Gang."

Reference: the Pyrotechnics Mailing List

HONORABLE MENTION: WELDING WARNING

Confirmed by Darwin

1 JANUARY 2004, SINGAPORE

If you ever find yourself with a leaking fuel tank on your motor-bike, be sure to heed this lesson from a thirty-nine-year-old man from the Bukit Panjang neighborhood. He removed the leaky tank from the bike and carried it to his sixth-floor flat, where he drained the gasoline into a pail in his toilet. Considering what happened next, it was fortunate that nobody else was in the flat, and that nobody was standing on manhole covers a block away.

He lit a propane torch, planning to solder the hole in the tank. Unfortunately, gasoline that had spilled on his hand caught fire. Frantically trying to extinguish the flames by plung-ing his hand into the toilet, he ignited the gasoline fumes com-ing from the pail. The toilet was engulfed in a ball of fire, and the explosion "shook the block." Smoke poured out of the bath-room window.

That was just the beginning. Some of the burning gasoline spilled down a floor drain and into the sewer system, where it mingled with sewer gas and set off a massive underground ex-plosion. Startled residents watched in amazement as one man-hole cover was "blown to pieces" and two others popped open. People fled their homes, fearing disaster.

The man survived all of this chaos with minor burns on his left hand, for which he refused treatment.

I'm Jumping Jack Flash—*Rolling Stones*

Reference: Channel NewsAsia, *Singapore Straits Times*

HONORABLE MENTION: CROTCH ROCKET

Confirmed by Darwin

28 MARCH 2004, JACKSONVILLE, FLORIDA

Jeremiah, thirty-five, had a fun idea for a prank: shoot a six-inch fireworks rocket at his girlfriend as he drove by in his Ford Mustang. But before he could launch it out the window, the fuse burned down to the ignition point, and the rocket began to ricochet around the inside of his car, finally exploding between his legs. The flash temporarily blinded him, which protected him from seeing the extent of the damage.

Neighbors saw the flash and heard the explosion. They rushed toward the car to find a person on fire! They extinguished the flames to reveal a man singed from his groin to his toes, with an outline of his sandals burned onto his feet.

"I thought I was dead," Jeremiah told a reporter. "I couldn't see, I couldn't hear, I couldn't walk." He was taken to a medical center and treated for second-degree burns. When interviewed by a reporter, he reflected on his potentially fatal encounter with rockets, raised his hairless eyebrows, and said, "No more of those!"

Reference: WJXT-TV, *Florida Times-Union*, AP

Honorable Mention: Hot Pants

Confirmed by Darwin
30 July 2004, Georgia

Gustav, thirty-nine, was hard at work in his laboratory when un-invited guests knocked on the door. Because his work was rather secret, he poured two of the chemicals, red phosphorus and io-dine, into an empty film cannister and stuffed it in his pocket be-fore going out to greet his visitors. They were two social workers bearing forms, and Gustav walked them out to their car, sat in the back seat, and began writing.

"He kept fiddling with his front right pants pocket," said the commander of the drug task force. The film cannister was probably feeling warm as the red phosphorus and iodine began to react. These chemicals are key ingredients in the making of methamphetamine. What Gustav apparently did not know was that the now-boiling mixture of red phosphorus and iodine would soon reach 278 degrees Fahrenheit.

"All of a sudden, a loud bang happened, and fire shot from his pocket. It damaged the inside of the state vehicle." Gustav suf-fered second- and third-degree burns to his testicles and leg. He was rushed to a medical center in Chattanooga, Tennessee, be-fore being hauled off to jail. Sheriff's deputies raided the house and discovered his meth lab. He was charged with the manufac-ture and possession of illegal drugs.

"That was one for the books," said a Walker County sheriff's spokesperson. "I've been in this business for more than thirty-five years, and that's a first."

Reference: *Atlanta Journal-Constitution*, foxnews.com

HONORABLE MENTION: EXPLODING BOAT

Confirmed by Darwin

11 APRIL 2004, POMPANO BEACH, FLORIDA

Bill, forty-four, and Ted, forty-seven, narrowly avoided earning a double Darwin when they accidentally blew up their fishing boat. They had stopped at a gas station to fill up the boat's gas tank. Unfortunately, they put the nozzle into one of the fishing-rod holders instead of the gas tank, sending fuel throughout the boat. With gasoline sloshing around in the bilge and forming a vapor cloud, the two men drove merrily on, looking forward to a great day of fishing.

They launched the boat, which floated quietly in the calm water—until they pushed the starter on the engine. The spark from the engine instantly ignited the vapor cloud surrounding the men. The force of the blast knocked them both to the deck. The twenty-six-foot boat was engulfed in flames and destroyed, along with part of the nearby dock. Firefighters spent ten minutes trying to control the blaze.

Bill was treated and released from the emergency room. Ted was transferred to the burn unit and released the next day. "It certainly was a horrible lesson to learn about boating," said the Pompano Beach Fire-Rescue spokesperson.

Reference: wftv.com, *Fort Lauderdale Sun-Sentinel, St. Petersburg Times*

HONORABLE MENTION: EXPLODING OUTHOUSE

Confirmed by Darwin

13 JULY 2004, BLACKSVILLE, WEST VIRGINIA

A man decided to light up a cigarette while relaxing in a portable outhouse, inadvertently demonstrating one more reason to give up the habit. According to a spokeswoman for Monongalia Emergency Medical Services, the methane in the Porta-Potty "didn't take too kindly" to the lit cigarette, and expressed its displeasure by exploding in a fireball.

The man, whose identity was withheld "due to privacy policies," was able to drive himself to a nearby health center. Emergency workers declined to reveal whether the man's injuries (although not "life-threatening") were serious enough to remove him from the gene pool.

Reference: *Dominion Post*

HONORABLE MENTION: FLAMING BUNGEE JUMP

Confirmed by Darwin

17 JANUARY 2004, BRISTOL, ENGLAND

The Clifton Suspension Bridge, soaring two hundred fifty feet above the seven-hundred-foot-wide Avon Gorge, has attracted people with something to prove ever since it was finished. In 1885 Sarah Ann Henley threw herself from the bridge after an argument with a boyfriend, but was saved by her parachute-like dress and cushiony crinoline petticoats. In 1957, a flying officer of the RAF successfully flew a Vampire jet under the bridge at four hundred fifty miles per hour. He briefly celebrated before he and his jet disintegrated on the cliffs on the south side.

To prevent further incidents, rules were established prohibiting under-flights, over-jumps, and other aberrant behavior. Bungee jumping is specifically banned. Despite strict rules, however, the historic bridge attracts many would-be Darwin candidates, such as Slim, twenty-two, who violated the rules and lived to tell the tale.

Slim walked onto the bridge, attached a lengthy bungee cord, and leapt off. His plan was to set himself on fire, cut the cord, and drop into the river below, quenching the flames. Unfortunately his knife was not up to the task. The blazing man dangled over the river for twenty-six interminable seconds, before he found a spare knife and severed the rope. At long last he plunged into the river, extinguishing the flames, and then swam off.

Slim was taken to the Bristol Royal Infirmary and later transferred to the burn unit in the city. A spokesperson for the Dangerous Sports Club told the BBC, "His heart is in the right place, but stunt men usually put on flame-retardant suits." Slim himself told the BBC that it was a thrill-seeking stunt that went horribly wrong. After that brief comment, he demanded £1,000 for a full interview.

Reference: BBC News On-Line

HONORABLE MENTION:
COOKING WITH GAS
Unconfirmed by Darwin
19 AUGUST 1991, CONNECTICUT

The good news as Hurricane Bob bore down on the Atlantic coast was that everybody in J.R.'s office was sent home early to prepare for the storm. And J.R. was well prepared. No matter how bad the devastation, he would have light, heat, water, and hot food. So he had nothing to worry about when the power failed under the massive onslaught of the storm.

The bad news was that, despite his thorough preparations, J.R. had forgotten one important detail.

As night fell, he fired up the oil lamps and placed his Coleman camping stove on top of the electric range in his kitchen to cook his dinner. After finishing the meal, J.R. commended himself on his foresight. He went to bed secure in the knowledge that Mother Nature could not beat him.

Diligent linemen worked through the worst of the weather to restore power. Before dawn, all the appliances in J.R.'s house were again working, including the electric range. But J.R. had forgotten to check that one important detail. . . .

The burner under the Coleman was on, heating the little stove's gas canister through the night. It finally exploded, blowing the kitchen wall two feet off the foundation, snapping several floor joists, and smashing every window in the house. The explosion caused $65,000 in damage, and J.R. had narrowly escaped an encounter with destiny—saved only by his closed bedroom door.

Reference: *New London Day*

Personal Account: Cleaning Solution
New York

Saul was a thirty-nine-year-old manager at a company that provides plasma to burn victims. He was also an avid snowmobiler. Early one morning on the way to work, he purchased some gasoline to use as a cleaning solution for the sled's engine. (There are so many ways that plan can go wrong—which will Saul choose?) He placed the container on the front seat of his car and went into work.

That afternoon, Saul needed to retrieve some paperwork from the car. Since smoking was not allowed in the building, it seemed an opportune moment to slide into the car and light up. But his cigarette wasn't the only thing that lit up when he flicked his Bic.

Fumes had been leaking from the gas container all day. As he took his first (and last) drag, they ignited. In the inferno, Saul's car was severely damaged, but he managed to escape with only a few burns, becoming one of the few to be eligible for his company's employee discount program for plasma!

Reference: Personal Account

PERSONAL ACCOUNT: TIGHT WAD
SUMMER 2003, ENGLAND

I am a key intensive-care staff member in Buckinghamshire. One summer day a patient was brought in, sirens screaming. The thirty-eight-year-old was obviously the victim of an explosion, with shrapnel wounds and gunpowder burns on his face and abdomen. His thigh and groin had also sustained serious injury, although his testicles were intact.

We removed a three-inch section of twisted pipe from his abdomen, repaired his large intestine, and sealed ruptured vessels to control bleeding. After five hours of surgery, the patient was admitted to the ICU on a ventilator and blood and plasma expanders.

The police thought he might be a terrorist whose bomb had detonated prematurely, and they placed a media restriction on him. Due to the restriction, the full details never appeared in the press, but the story started to emerge when we spoke to the man's brother-in-law.

The victim was not a terrorist at all, but an unemployed van driver. During a family get-together, he took his thirteen-year-old nephew down to his brother-in-law's garden shed for a fishing lesson. To catch fish at the local quarry, he planned to teach the boy a technique he had pioneered in his youth: tossing homemade explosives into the lake and collecting the stunned fish that floated to the surface.

This clever fisherman cut a section of five centimeters scaffolding pipe and hammered one end closed. Then he packed it with a pad of cotton, rammed home with a smaller section of steel pipe. On top of this he poured a substantial amount of gunpowder taken from bootleg Chinese aerial fireworks, which are illegal in the U.K. His plan was to place another cotton pad on top of the gunpowder and seal the whole bundle with a plug of wood.

Considerable hammering and noise were required to get a "tight wad." As it was Sunday, the brother-in-law was worried that the neighbors would complain about the noise. Twice he asked his relative to cease and desist, and finally took his son and proceeded back toward the house.

Meanwhile, this Darwin candidate continued to ram home the pipe's contents while holding the device between his legs for stability. As the gentleman explained to me some weeks later, "My big mistake was when I used the steel pipe to pack the tube, instead of the end of the wooden hammer-handle."

Indeed. The brother-in-law and his son were thirty feet from the shed when a spark ignited the gunpowder.

The pipe bomb shot the wooden plug into his eye orbit, whilst the body of the pipe unwrapped like a cardboard tube and launched itself into the gentleman's abdomen. The blunt lateral force stopped the pipe from ejecting from his body, but the impact lacerated his bowels and the shock force and shrapnel caused massive hemorrhaging.

The candidate lost a major part of his thigh, but the upward force of the explosion protected his testicles from injury, so his genes were not lost to humanity. He survived the incident, and has therefore not quite fulfilled the full Darwin Award criteria, although the facial disfigurement may yet ensure that his genes are not propagated.

One comment made the trauma team's day. The surgeon displayed a three-inch metal fragment from the man's abdomen and announced to all and sundry, "Who's going to contact the Darwin Awards, then?" All four doctors, three nurses, and two technicians cracked up laughing. Medical humor!

Reference: Ches Whistler, Personal Account

PERSONAL ACCOUNT: MEDIEVAL FLAMBÉ
SPRING 1992, BOWLING GREEN, KENTUCKY

The Society for Creative Anachronism was re-creating medieval life at Beech Bend Park, which is nestled in a woody curve of the Barren River. Two female friends had pitched their tents with other sword-wielding, baggy-pants celebrants. They invited me and "Adam" to join them for one evening's campout. Since both were lovely blondes, as well as charming companions, we readily agreed. They provided us with faux-medieval garb that would enable us to blend into the crowd. A tabard and baggy pants were enough for me, but Adam wanted something more.

Every SCAdian practices a skill, be it cooking, dancing, craft, or energetically whacking others with a duct-taped sword. Adam wanted to go all the way. He can juggle, which was a start, but not quite impressive enough. He decided to breathe fire. Adam had seen this stunt performed with pure grain alcohol. But he'd never done it, he was too young to buy alcohol, and the liquor stores closed at eleven P.M. Still determined to blaze with glory, he went looking for a substitute.

Let's see . . . what flammable liquids can a young man buy in a Kentucky Wal-Mart at eleven-thirty P.M.? There were several choices, none good. Adam settled on Coleman stove fuel. It was clear, and it didn't smell too bad. He could pour it into an empty wine bottle for period realism. Adam decided it was close enough.

Back at camp, Adam told one blonde friend, "C'mere, I've go something to show you" and led her behind a large cloth tent. Nearby stood a group of men in chain-mail armor, warming themselves around a fire. They could see Adam, but I couldn't.

Seconds later, a deep "WHOOOM!" burst from behind the tent, accompanied by a gout of orange flame. "Whoa!" cried al the guys around the campfire, turning to applaud. But their ap plause soon died. Through a double layer of tent fabric I could see this . . . afterglow. "Holy shit! He's on fire!" the mail-clad men yelled, and ran over to pound out the flames blazing around Adam's head.

What Adam hadn't realized was that unlike grain alcohol stove fuel gives off copious fumes. As he swigged the fuel, some trickled down his chin. Fortunately, he'd shaved off his goatee the day before. As it was, fumes wreathed his head and fue trickled down his throat. In the ensuing conflagration, he man aged to scorch his eyebrows and the hair off the back of hi head, while hardly touching that on top. Rivulets of flame rar down his neck, and he suffered chemical burns in his throat.

Adam was still standing, and at first thought he was not seri ously hurt. But the burns started to sting, and I led him to the chirurgeon's tent. They quickly ascertained that neither me dieval technology nor modern first aid would suffice, and I drove Adam to the hospital in a horseless carriage. The burns on hi neck healed without serious scarring, his hair regrew, and the octave he lost off his voice came back in about six months.

Five years later, I went to another SCA gathering in a differ ent city, accompanying the same female friends. A long and en tertaining day concluded with a belly-dancing demonstratior around a bonfire, accompanied by throbbing drums. I turned to the stranger standing next to me and commented on how exciting the event was.

"Aw, this is nothin', man," he replied. "If you think this is exciting, you shoulda been here five years ago. Some crazy dude set his head on fire!"

Reference: Jim Gaines, Personal Account

PERSONAL ACCOUNT: POCKET M80
2002, CANADA

In my small community, news travels fast, but it doesn't usually travel far. This is an event that I witnessed but still can't believe. My friend "Pyro" is a moron and a firebug, like every other boy in high school. His father was an avid hunter who loaded his own shells, so Pyro always had an ample supply of materials to satisfy his obsession.

One day after school, I noticed a group of kids huddled around Pyro. He had filled a small, heavy-duty cardboard tube with FFFF powder, which is used for black powder rifles. The tube was sealed with a generous amount of duct tape and had a crude wick protruding from the side.

Pyro pulled out his butane lighter, instructed everyone to step back, and lit the wick. But instead of doing the natural thing—throwing the crude M80 as fast and far as possible—he placed it between his legs right below his crotch, while he stowed the lighter back in his pocket.

The wick burned much too fast, and before he could grab it and hurl it, the explosive blew up between his legs. Pyro fell to the ground screaming, and when the dust cleared, we all expected to see a gigantic hole in his midsection. But we were astonished to find the tube in almost perfect condition, with the exception of two missing ends. There wasn't even a rip in his jeans.

Luckily for Pyro, he hadn't properly taped the explosive, and most of its force was released forward and aft. But unluckily for him, the explosion directed a certain amount of pressure against his testicles. Pyro managed to make it home and change his pants, and he told his mother he fell while walking along the top of a fence, thereby avoiding trouble over playing with explosives.

That happened ten years ago. During a trip home for Thanksgiving, I ran into Pyro, and it seems that he is unable to have children.

Reference: Paul Quattro, Personal Account

CHAPTER 7

Weapons

Whether wielded on the right side of the law, the wrong side, or no side of the law at all, weapons tend to bite the hand that feeds them. Guns, grenades, knives, bullets, and axes all hold a grudge against those who abuse them. But first, an essay about the forensic analysis of crime scenes. . . .

DISCUSSION:
FORENSIC ANALYSIS: ACHIEVING JUSTICE

Maia Smith, Science Writer

I magine that you are deciding whether to admit a certain type of evidence into court on a criminal case. You know that this type of evidence:

- Convicts innocent and guilty people with roughly the same frequency.*
- Is extremely susceptible to contamination from outside sources, e.g., through the method of retrieval.
- Was a key factor in convicting 60 percent of five hundred wrongly sentenced people who were later exonerated by DNA evidence, although it was used in only about 5 percent of cases.†
- Is highly trusted by jurors, who often believe it even if they know the sample is worthless.

What kind of evidence is this? It's eyewitness testimony, and it is a keystone of our justice system. Certainly eyewitness

*http://www.visualexpert.com/Resources/mistakenid.html
†Huff, C. Ronald. 2003. "Wrongful Conviction: Causes and Public Policy Issues." *Criminal Justice* Spring 2003, 18 (1).

testimony is deeply flawed and has led to many wrongful convictions. For every innocent man in jail, a guilty one runs free. If this were a new high-tech method, like analyzing fiber or DNA, it would have been abandoned as soon as the statistics became known. Yet no human rights activist would dream of advocating for a ban on eyewitness identification in court, despite its low rate of accuracy.

Study after study shows that memory is extremely unreliable and subject to tampering.* Witnesses can be misled by weapon focus, preexisting biases, being shown a lineup of suspects rather than one picture at a time (they tend to pick the person in the lineup most similar to the perpetrator), being questioned by a biased interrogator such as an attorney, and so forth. And bear in mind that studies of witness inaccuracy are done in a controlled setting that tends to decrease the error: None of the study witnesses were offered leniency in exchange for testimony, or had a loaded gun pointed at them while making observations.

The problems with eyewitness testimony are exacerbated in the case of repressed memories. Therapists claim that people subconsciously close off memories that are too painful to live with. This theory is undermined by the vivid accounts of Holocaust survivors and other torture victims. Therapists can sometimes "retrieve" repressed memories, although some techniques generate false memories just as easily.† The sketchy reliability of such memories has not stopped the use of

*http://www.psy.mq.edu.au/staff/kip/PL7.htm has most of the eyewitness-inaccuracy info, plus more references.
†Sagan, Carl. *The Demon-Haunted World: Science as a Candle in the Dark*. Ballantine Books, 1997.

this testimony in court, and many innocent people have been jailed after someone claimed horrific abuse (usually sexual) that occurred so long ago that an alibi or defense is unlikely.*
Jurors, being human, shy away from flatly contradicting a sobbing witness, even if the evidence proves she is deluded.

How does DNA evidence compare to eyewitness testimony?

DNA analysis garnered good press in the 1990s, when it exonerated people who were wrongly sentenced to life in prison. Suddenly, a drinking glass or comb had the potential to identify its user beyond a reasonable doubt. Paternity cases became open-and-shut, as did cases of forcible rape.†

DNA analysis is extremely accurate.† Errors are so rare (1 in 10,000) that DNA, if available, is nearly always the most accurate method of identification. Problems with DNA analysis are nearly always low-tech, caused by a careless worker. Even a good lab has an error rate of 1 in 200, not because of inaccuracy in the DNA testing itself, but because, for example, samples are mislabeled or contaminated.

This is not a problem if DNA tests are performed after there is reason to suspect a person. However, with the growth of DNA databases, the possibility now exists for someone to be accused based solely on DNA. This creates a measurable risk of a false identification. For example, processing a rape kit often takes years. A scan through a database of DNA profiles could lead to a chance hit on an innocent person who cannot remember what he was doing on the night of September 17, 2002. A false positive rate of 1 in 200 may be acceptable if there

*"Recovered Memories: Recent Events and Review of Evidence." Interview with Harrison G. Pope Jr., M.D. *Currents in Affective Illness,* XIII (7), July 1994, 5–12.
†DNA analysis is commonly claimed to be 99.99% accurate. http://www.dost. gov.ph/media/article.php?sid=488

are three suspects, two of whom are likely to be eliminated by DNA analysis; it is not acceptable when randomly combing through the linked databases of the FBI and various states, which currently contain close to two million DNA profiles.

DNA's extremely high accuracy rate can also lead to misinterpretation. We may prove beyond a reasonable doubt that the defendant has the murder victim's blood on his shirt, without proving anything at all about whether he participated in the murder. He might have simply bandaged her skinned knee earlier that day. There have already been five cases of identical twins implicated in a crime that only one committed* (although in only one case has there been any difficulty eliminating the innocent twin from suspicion). A 99.5% chance that the test has correctly identified a bloodstain does not translate into a 99.5% chance that the defendant is guilty, but the jury might give the evidence unwarranted weight. Likewise, an attorney might mention the low error rate of a test, without mentioning that the immense database almost guarantees a few chance hits. The problem isn't with DNA evidence per se, but with how it's presented in the courtroom and interpreted by the jury.

So let's examine how the jury trial itself can err.

Juries weigh evidence differently than logic would dictate. Facts, figures, graphs, and experts convey information, but may confuse the jury. Eyewitnesses and vivid descriptions grab attention and sympathy, but often convey no new information. Juries will convict on the basis of eyewitness testimony

*USA Today, posted June 3, 2004, by Richard Willing, describes a few problems with identical twins. http://www.usatoday.com/news/nation/2004-06-03-twins-dna_x.htm

two-thirds of the time, even if the only witness wasn't wearing his glasses. Without a witness, they convict only one-sixth of the time.* A jury is more likely to believe a confident witness than a hesitant one, even though tests prove that confidence does not correlate with witness accuracy. Juries might acquit due to sympathy. And they're more likely to convict if the crime was particularly horrendous, even if it's not clear who committed it.

Forensic analysis is a clash between science and emotion. We have a huge array of tools for analyzing the tiniest shreds of evidence: bloodstains, fibers, bullets, and even repressed memories. At the same time, these are only tools. They can be used for justice or injustice. They can clarify the facts, or simply muddy the waters. Cutting through the gory details and tech-talk still requires a dispassionate, intelligent human mind—the first, last, and only tool we've ever had for achieving justice.

A jury trial is one potential payoff for the misuse of a weapon, but an even more formidable trial is that of natural selection. In the following stories, misused weapons themselves act as judge and jury to mete out their own form of justice. . . .

---

*http://www.psy.mq.edu.au/staff/kip/PL7.htm has most of the eyewitness-inaccuracy info, plus more references.

Darwin Award: Surprise Attack Surprise

Confirmed by Darwin

3 January 2005, St. Maurice im Wallis, Switzerland

It was the first week of a weapons refresher course, and Swiss Army Grenadier Detachment 20/5 had just finished training with live ammunition. The shooting instructor ordered the soldiers to secure their weapons for a break.

The twenty-four-year-old second lieutenant in charge of this detachment decided this would be a good time to demonstrate a knife attack on a soldier. Wielding his bayonet, he leapt toward one of his men, achieving complete surprise.

But earlier that week, the soldiers had been drilled to release the safety catch and ready their guns for firing in the shortest possible time. The surprised soldier, seeing his lieutenant leaping toward him with a knife, snapped off a shot to protect himself from the attack.

The lesson could not have been more successful: The soldier had saved himself and protected the rest of the detachment from a surprise attack. The lieutenant might have wished to commend his soldier on his quick action and accurate marksmanship. Unfortunately, he had been killed with one shot.

And this, kiddies, is why we don't play with knives or guns. Ever. Even if we are trained professionals, and especially if our target is a trained professional.   Reference: Blick

Reader Comments:

"No one brings knives to paintball this weekend!!!"

"That's what he gets for bringing a knife to a gun fight!"

DARWIN AWARD: EXPLODING EX-TORTIONIST

Confirmed by Darwin

7 SEPTEMBER 2003, PHNOM PENH, CAMBODIA

Khim, nicknamed "The Big Giant," was an intimidatingly large former military policeman when he arrived at the home of a drug dealer to extort money and amphetamines. He was a much smaller man soon afterward.

He pulled the pin from a grenade to threaten the dealer, who immediately decided to give him the items he demanded. Then Khim, who had been drinking, forgot to put the pin back before slipping the grenade into his pocket.

He walked to his motorbike, well satisfied with the transaction. As he climbed aboard, the grenade exploded. Whether the drug dealer recovered his cash (and in what condition!) is unknown.

Reference: AAP, news.com.au, *The Daily News* (South Africa)

DARWIN AWARD: SHOOTING BLANKS
Confirmed by Darwin
11 MARCH 2003, MADRID, SPAIN

Early one morning, police received a call. Three robbers had invaded a brothel! Officers surrounded the building and used a bullhorn to coax the offenders from the premises.

The robbers were understandably frightened to be surrounded by dozens of policemen. But instead of surrendering, they decided to go out in a blaze of glory, and fled the building while shooting at everything in sight. The policemen ducked, covered, and shot back. Two running robbers were fatally injured, and the third was wounded.

Why was the gunfight over so quickly? The three robbers were carrying REAL guns loaded with FAKE ammunition. They were firing blanks, making enough flash and thunder to fool the police into shooting back, but not enough to actually help them escape.

Reference: www.terra.es, Terra Networks, South America

HONORABLE MENTION: SHOOT 'EM OFF
Confirmed by Darwin
7 MAY 2002, WISCONSIN

"For being named Lantern, he sure wasn't very bright."

Lantern, thirty, enjoyed playing a private game with his wife. He would pull down his pants, place the barrel of a shotgun against his scrotum, and tell her to pull the trigger. They had played this game frequently, to his immense pleasure. The gun was unloaded, of course.

On this pleasant Friday, he was excited to try again. The thrill was even larger because his wife's girlfriend was pulling into the driveway at the time. "Shoot 'em off before she gets here!" Lantern told his wife. She pulled the trigger. But this time, the gun was loaded.

Emergency crews arrived to find Lantern bleeding profusely from his groin, wearing shoes and socks, with his pants down around his ankles. The police were told it was an accident, and the couple didn't know the gun was loaded. Lantern was admitted to the hospital in critical condition, where he survived, possibly earning the right to the rarest of honors: the Living Darwin Award. We await confirmation of his procreative status.

Reference: *Green Bay Press-Gazette*

DARWIN AWARD: SLAUGHTERHOUSE ROBBERY

Unconfirmed by Darwin

12 FEBRUARY 2003, THE NETHERLANDS

Three men wielding knives tried to rob a slaughterhouse (for what, we wonder). But when it comes to hand-to-hand combat with sharp blades, butchers working in a slaughterhouse are more than a match for your average knife-wielding thief. They stabbed two of the intruders to death. The third man escaped from the angry butchers and fled in his car.

Police soon spotted him, and after a brief car chase, the would-be thief pulled over and leapt from his vehicle. But instead of fleeing into the underbrush, he tried to dodge heavy traffic and escape across the highway. Perhaps he thought that threatening butchers with knives was not a sufficient demonstration of his intelligence.

Within seconds, the natural justice system meted out his punishment in the form of a large truck, which struck and killed him.

Reference: Eyewitness account

DARWIN AWARD: SHARP LANDING

Unconfirmed by Darwin
FEBRUARY 2003, DILI, EAST TIMOR

"A do-it-yourself briss (circumcision)."

A man was found lying facedown, covered in mud and blood, the apparent victim of a street crime. It was not until a post-mortem examination was conducted that U.N. police were able to reconstruct his last moments, based on an unusual discovery in his pants.

> **Safety Tip: If you're ever stuck with a knife, DON'T PULL IT OUT!** It may be painful, but it's acting as a plug for your wound. Pull the knife out, and you're left with a hole ready to leak whatever's inside out.

This up-and-coming young man decided it was cool to shove his weapons, two long knives, down the waistband of his trousers. Unsheathed. The hapless fellow jumped over a small fence and landed in a large puddle of mud. He slipped, which sent the blade of his "trouser knife" into his leg and severed his femoral artery. This has the same effect as cutting off the bottom of a paper cup filled with water. In thirty seconds, one loses enough blood to be rendered unconscious, with nearly complete blood loss within two minutes. He bled to death before he could stagger ten feet from the puddle.

HONORABLE MENTION:
NIGHTTIME FUN WITH BULLETS

Confirmed by Darwin

25 MARCH 2005, SALINA, KANSAS

"At the time, he was uncooperative," said the Saline County sheriff, describing the difficulty deputies encountered in finding the cause of a self-inflicted bullet wound. Perhaps Lou, the twenty-seven-year-old victim of his inner klutz, was simply embarrassed to admit he had managed to shoot himself in the groin with a .22-caliber bullet—while armed only with a pellet gun.

The deputy's report included no mention of alcohol, so Lou was apparently sober when he placed a bullet on a picnic table and fired at it with his air rifle. The results he expected are not known. But the experiment yielded conclusive data. As he eventually, and abashedly, explained to a detective, "a pellet from the rifle hit the shell, causing it to explode."

The bullet shot into his groin, fragmenting into an area rich with major nerves and arteries, thereby presenting an interesting challenge to Kansas City neurosurgeons. They were up to the task, and Lou was thereby deprived of winning a full Darwin Award . . . this time!

Reference: *Salina Journal*

HONORABLE MENTION: BAKED BULLET SURPRISE

Confirmed by Darwin

17 FEBRUARY 2004, HOWARD, WISCONSIN

Just as squirrels bury their acorns to protect them from predators for later use, a man from Howard put his ammunition and three handguns in a safe place before he and his wife departed on vacation. He wanted to be sure they would be there when the couple returned. But just as squirrels frequently forget where they buried a particular acorn, the man forgot that his hiding place was the oven. When they returned from their trip, his wife turned on the oven to prepare dinner. Shortly afterward the couple had to duck behind the refrigerator as the bullets began to explode like popcorn. The husband used a fire extinguisher to put out the fire that the bullets started in the oven. No humans were hurt, but the prognosis for the oven was grim.

Reference: *Minneapolis Star Tribune*

HONORABLE MENTION: SELF-PROTECTION
Confirmed by Darwin
28 NOVEMBER 2004, IDAHO

Police found Camero lying on the floor behind his bar, bleeding from a gunshot wound. A .22-caliber revolver lay on the floor nearby. The cash register was open, but the cash was undisturbed. It appeared that the bar owner had bravely fended off a robbery attempt—but looks can be deceiving!

Actually, the man had brought his gun along for protection when he unloaded the Saturday-night revenue from the cash register. Camero had trouble getting the register drawer open, so he tucked the gun under his arm and applied a bit more force. The gun slipped, hit the floor, and shot him through the groin, narrowly missing his reproductive organs and his heart before lodging in his right chest cavity.

But at least the cash was safe!

4 AUGUST 2004, OKLAHOMA

In a similar incident, law enforcement officers called off their search for an escaped prisoner in order to help a gunshot victim. The victim had been carrying a .22-caliber pistol in the waistband of his cutoff jeans to protect himself from an escaped prisoner he had heard about. To be extra safe, he had pulled back the hammer of the gun before putting it into his pants. The gun went off and shot him in the left buttock. The victim admitted that the incident was "one of my most embarrassing moments." The escapee remained at large.

Reference: *Spokane Spokesman-Review,* AP

HONORABLE MENTION:
TESTOSTERONE, CHICKENS, AND GUNS
Confirmed by Darwin
10 DECEMBER 2004, WASHINGTON

Not far from the Eastern Washington State Hospital for the mentally handicapped, Donnie, an eighteen-year-old A student in gun-safety classes, decided to impress his girlfriend with his coyote hunting skills. He needed a live chicken as bait. So, girlfriend in one hand and .22-caliber rifle in the other, he entered the butchering barn where carefree chickens roamed.

You never know how a mix of testosterone, chickens, and guns will turn out. There are so many variables.

Donnie climbed into the attic, intending to use the stock of the rifle as a club. He swung the rifle at a fluttering fowl, but the rafters got in the way. The gun butt hit the ceiling and discharged, sending a bullet into his right forearm and out the elbow. He didn't realize he had shot himself until he noticed his right hand twitching, and took his coat off for a closer look.

Donnie shared the lesson he learned: "To know you shot yourself and came close to dying, it's a pretty scary deal. You've gotta be careful with guns."

Reference: *Spokane Spokesman-Review*

PERSONAL ACCOUNT: VILLAGE IDIOT

2003, CALIFORNIA

I am what is known as a "Rennie," or Renaissance fair participant. We are a close-knit bunch, and nobody's secrets are safe for long. So it's no secret who the village idiot is. When God was passing out brains, Tim must have thought he said "trains" and requested HO scale. Really.

Because it's a Renaissance festival, we sell what we refer to as "sharp pointy things." Several booths are dedicated to knives and swords of all sorts. At one particular booth, Knightware, they sell sharp little throwing knives called spiders. Larger blades are not sold with a live edge for safety reasons; however, small knives are not only sharpened, but usually better made.

A customer who was interested in blades came across the Knightware spiders. When he asked if they were sharp, Tim replied, "No, look," and drove the one-inch blade straight into his chest with all the force he could muster.

If it had been a cheap knife, it would have come out easily, but the well-made little blade lodged tight in Tim's sternum. Tim was driven to the hospital, where the spider was removed. He was subsequently billed for the knife, on the grounds that no one else wanted to buy a knife with its bloodthirsty history.

Tim was taken back to the hospital two weeks later to stitch his thumb together. He had been sharpening his new knife when it slipped, and he cut himself down to the bone. Tim is now banned from all weapons stalls, although he doesn't understand why.

Reference: Personal Account

Most "Renfaires" require weapons to be "peace tied" to prevent injury.

More information on this story:

www.DarwinAwards.com/book/rennie.html

PERSONAL ACCOUNT: GUN-SAFETY NONSENSE
MID-1980S, SEATTLE, WASHINGTON

I worked with a man who taught hunting skills and gun safety after hours. He came to work one day visibly shaken and told this story.

As his teenage students gathered around him, he warned them not to trust the safety switch of the gun, telling them that it could fail. One of the students did not show up for class for the next few weeks, and then came in (the night before I heard this story) to tell the instructor how his father had died. The student had gone home after his last class, and told his father about not trusting the safety. The father became irate that the instructor would teach such nonsense. He proceeded to load a rifle, flip the safety on, and hit the butt of the stock on the floor to prove the instructor wrong. Unfortunately, the instructor turned out to be right, while the father was fatally mistaken. The gun went off and killed the man.

Reference: Personal Account

PERSONAL ACCOUNT:
DO WHAT I SAY, NOT WHAT I DO
CA. 1961, USA

When I was a Boy Scout, one of our troop leaders decided to teach us how to use an axe safely. Of course, this was after we were shown how to sharpen an axe to a razor edge. A dull blade is the most dangerous weapon.

The safety demonstration was going well until he decided to show us how dangerous it would be to strike a log with a glancing blow. We all watched in amazement as he took a mighty swing with the axe and struck the log with a glancing blow. The axe bounced off the log and buried itself in his left kneecap. Since it was summertime and he was wearing shorts, this turned out to be a very graphic demonstration.

Fortunately, he missed all major arteries, but he did chop his kneecap in half and had to be rushed to the hospital for emergency surgery. He walked with a limp after that. It was the best demonstration of axe safety I ever saw.

Reference: John Stein, Personal Account; Blick

CHAPTER 8

Miscellaneous

Some innovative Darwin Awards don't fall into predictable categories. Enjoy the miscellaneous methods man has invented to bedevil himself, using thallium, an ice maker, trees, scaffolding, a confession, a nail gun, a homemade parachute, chocolate sauce, electromagnets, an innocent paper-towel dispenser, or an auger—two different ways. But first, get ready to make friends with your worst enemy in a scientific discussion of fat. . . .

Discussion: The Skinny on Fat

Annaliese Beery, Science Writer

Most people hate fat—some even die getting rid of it (for instance, by garage liposuction).* The death rate in liposuction surgery is twenty to sixty times the death rate of all hospital operations, and 2 percent of gastric-bypass patients die within a few months of surgery. As sobering as these statistics are, they are dwarfed by the death toll from fat's indirect consequences: clogged arteries, high blood pressure, and heart disease—the most common cause of death in the United States. So it may come as a surprise that fat is one of the most useful molecules in your body. Without fat you wouldn't have enough energy to sleep through the night! With a whopping nine calories per gram, fats (also called lipids) are the most efficient storage molecule in your body, containing large amounts of energy in a small space. When babies are born with a disease that prevents them from digesting fats, they must be awakened at regular intervals to be fed nonfatty foods, or kept on IV glucose, or else they will run out of energy between meals. Failure to metabolize fat is one of the causes of Sudden

*www.DarwinAwards.com/book/liposuction.html

Infant Death Syndrome, where apparently healthy babies die inexplicably during the night.

You need fats as a day-to-day energy carrier, too. Just consider what it would take to live without them: In order to carry the amount of energy using protein or carbohydrates, a 70-kilogram (154-pound) person would have to weigh more than 100 kilograms (220 pounds). And that extra weight would not be nearly as cushioning and insulating as fat.

Structure Leads to Function:
Making Margarine

Fat's high energy comes from its molecular structure. Like wax and gasoline, lipids consist of long chains of carbon and hydrogen that can be slowly "burned" by your body to yield energy, water, and carbon dioxide. Lipids come in different lengths and can be saturated or unsaturated, which affects the shape of the chain and what it does in your body.

Each carbon atom in a lipid chain can hold up to two hydrogens, and a saturated fat is full of them. In unsaturated fat, double bonds between carbons replace some of the hydrogens. If there is one double bond, the fat is monounsaturated. Polyunsaturated fats have multiple double bonds and fewer hydrogens.

Saturation in fats: what a difference a bond makes!

Simplified view of a lipid (actual lipids are longer, and have more variety on one end). The black balls represent carbon atoms (4 bonds each) and the white balls represent hydrogen atoms (1 bond each). This carbon chain is fully saturated with hydrogen.

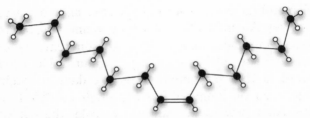

The resulting shape if the carbon chain loses two hydrogens from one side and replaces them with a double bond. Because the lipid is no longer full of hydrogens it is unsaturated, and it has a kinked shape.

Saturated animal fats, like butter and lard, are solid at room temperature because the flat fat molecules pack together tightly and stick to each other. Vegetable fats are generally unsaturated and full of double bonds, giving them a kinked molecular shape; they don't pack together well and remain liquid, so you have to keep them in a bottle.

If you want your vegetable oil to be solid, like margarine, you can either chill it or get rid of the kinks by adding hydrogens. Voila! Partially hydrogenated vegetable oils have more single bonds and are solid at room temperature.

Saturation also plays a role in your arteries, where different shapes of fat flow differently through the blood. Kinked, unsaturated fats don't stick to blood vessels, because blood pushes against their exposed surface and moves them along to where they are needed. Saturated fats, on the other hand, lie flat and occasionally stick to the sides of blood vessels, forming arteriosclerotic plaques. Autopsies of healthy soldiers show that a man in his mid-twenties has usually lost an astonishing 30 percent of the diameter of his large arteries to fatty plaques!

Our cell membranes are made of lipids, too, and once again saturation is key. A combination of saturated and unsaturated lipids allows membranes to be semifluid at room temperature, but they are prone to solidify at cold temperatures, like bacon grease stored in the refrigerator. Frostbite damage begins when oxygen can no longer diffuse through solidified cell membranes. After prolonged exposure to cold, the coldest, outermost cells may die.

So why don't reindeer get frostbite? After all, they live in the arctic, and reindeer get seriously cold feet! The chemical structure of cell membranes in a reindeer leg shows an amazing adaptation: As you progress down the leg toward the hoof, a higher percentage of the lipids in the cell membranes are unsaturated, so they can stay fluid at very low temperatures.

Transport: Oil and Water Don't Mix

Anyone who's made salad dressing knows that fats don't dissolve in water, and they don't dissolve well in your blood, either. Organisms solve this problem with fat chaperones, which are large, water-soluble proteins called lipoproteins. Fats are

stored in your body as triglycerides, which are made up of three lipids. When a lipoprotein reaches a target cell, triglycerides must be broken apart into their component lipid chains, pulled across the cell membrane, and reassembled inside.

Fats also travel in the reverse direction—out of storage in fatty tissue and into circulation—to provide energy for other cells. If fat gets mobilized from storage and isn't used, it simply circulates until it is reincorporated into a fat cell. But during the time it spends in circulation, it has a small chance of adhering to an artery wall, potentially causing a heart attack or stroke. Doctors would like to know what makes this artery-clogger mobilize.

Your body's fat cells respond to cues that indicate the body is low on energy, or that the body is about to need more energy than usual. One of these cues is adrenaline, released as part of a stress response. While this stress response is not necessarily useful in an office job, in nature it prepares you to run or fight, so adrenaline mobilizes fat for action. Caffeine has many of the same effects as adrenaline. For this reason, marathon runners often consume caffeine an hour before they begin a race; this puts fat into the bloodstream so athletes can begin burning it for fuel as soon as they begin running. This helps their carbohydrate supply last longer. With only fat to rely on for energy, a runner will feel sluggish and low on energy. Without a caffeine boost, they "hit the wall" earlier and get stuck burning only fat, which is slower to metabolize than carbohydrates.

Most people who drink caffeine are not preparing for a marathon, so the circulating fat doesn't do much good. Consider, for example, a pilot's workday. During takeoff, one of the more stressful parts of a flight, his adrenaline levels are high, resulting in elevated fat circulation. If he drinks coffee first, his circulating fat levels will be even higher. Unlike the marathon runner, though, he'll sit for hours on end, causing fat to circulate without a target before ultimately returning to his fat cells. This losing combination means it's a good thing pilots are required to get an electrocardiogram every year after age forty.

If energy is the currency your body uses to perform its functions, then fat is a savings account. It's bad to have large amounts in circulation in your blood, but fat cells are a great way to store energy that will ultimately be converted into other forms, spent, or hoarded for a rainy day. Given how essential fats are, it's a shame they have such a bad reputation. Still, a gallon of ice cream will probably do you more harm than good.

REFERENCES:

Lipid reactivity to stress: Stoney, Catherine M.; Niaura, Raymond; Bausserman, Linda; Matacin, Mala. 1999. "Comparison of chronic and acute stress responses in middle-aged airline pilots." *Health Psychology*. Vol. 18(3) 241–250.

Hazel, J.R.; Williams, E.E. 1990. *Prog Lipid Res* 29(3):167–227. "The role of alterations in membrane lipid composition in enabling physiological adaptation of organisms to their physical environment."

Senault, C.; Yazbeck, J.; Goubern, M.; Portet, R.; Vincent, M.; Gallay, J. 1990. "Relation between membrane phospholipid composition, fluidity and function in mitochondria of rat brown adipose tissue. Effect of thermal adaptation and essential fatty acid deficiency." *Biochim Biophys Acta* 1023(2):283–289.

This final chapter contains a hodgepodge of stories, with one underlying theme: They are all examples that one should avoid emulating, if one wants to keep the body's metabolism running efficiently—or running at all!

DARWIN AWARD: WATCH OUT FOR THAT TREE!

Unconfirmed by Darwin

11 MAY 2004, STELLENBOSCH, SOUTH AFRICA

The mighty oak trees of Stellenbosch, a city near Cape Town, were planted more than three hundred years ago. In recent years, they have begun to succumb to disease. The city has been cutting them down and planting new trees.

A man was sitting at a café, watching a team with loud chain saws working to remove a tree whose center had become dangerously decayed. The arborists had marked the danger zone with red-and-white barrier tape and posted notices of danger, taking every precaution to prevent damage to property or persons.

Just as the tree was ready to fall, and the chain-saw operator was making the final cut, our man jumped up from his seat in the café. He ducked under the safety tape and started hurrying up the pavement to meet his girlfriend at a nearby shop. Despite the workers' frantic shouts, he continued toward the tree that by this time was falling as planned.

The chain-saw operator tried a desperate tackle to get him out the way, but it was too late. Missing the would-be rescuer by inches, the tree landed on the man's head, killing him instantly. And that is how one can qualify for a Darwin Award simply by walking under a tree.

Reference: *Eikestad Nuus*

DARWIN AWARD: BANNISTER TO HEAVEN

Confirmed by Darwin

20 JULY 2004, TALLAHASSEE, FLORIDA

The Kleman Plaza parking garage has the ideal bannister for a long slide, spiraling around an open stairwell all the way down from the fifth floor without a break. Brian, twenty-four, was a real-life hero who had saved a friend from drowning, but friends said he was also a "big fan of reality TV and high-risk stunts." The bannister was his big chance!

But just sliding down a five-story bannister was nowhere near risky enough for Brian, so he planned to leap onto the bannister to begin his slide. He ran, he jumped . . . and he sailed completely over it, plunging fifty-two feet to the bottom of the stairwell. A friend fondly reminisced that "Brian had done crazier things than this" before. But this was Brian's first stunt spectacular enough to win a Darwin Award.

According to a police investigation, "alcohol may have been a factor."

Reference: *Tallahassee Democrat*, WCTV

DARWIN AWARD: FLYING DUTCHMAN

Unconfirmed by Darwin

8 APRIL 2004, THE NETHERLANDS

The Martinitower is the tallest building in the north part of The Netherlands, rising ninety-six meters above the polders. High winds blast the top, making it a frightening place for some sightseers. Fortunately, a balustrade protects visitors from accidentally being blown off, and built-in seats allow them to rest their weary bodies after the onerous climb to the top. But these safety measures were mere inconveniences to a twenty-year-old man who decided to impress his girlfriend with his devil-may-care nonchalance. He climbed up on the balustrade and swung his legs to the outside. Then, aided by a gust of wind, he "slipped away," according to his father, who added, "he just liked to show off a little."

Reference: *Algemeen Dagblad*

DARWIN AWARD: CAUGHT IN THE AUGER

Unconfirmed by Darwin

31 JULY 1995, CHRISTCHURCH, NEW ZEALAND

"Welcome to the Machine."—Pink Floyd

An ice maker may seem innocuous, but when it's big enough to walk into—for example, one that supplies ice to fishing boats—it can be so dangerous that safety procedures and fail-safe devices are required. So it was a bit of a surprise when employees at a fish-processing plant heard screams emanating from inside the giant ice maker.

An employee had been running the machine when the flow of ice jammed. Access to the machine's auger chamber was restricted, and employees are trained never to enter the chamber while the auger is running. It would be easy enough to ignore the warning signs, but it is hard to get around another safety feature: The auger will not run unless the operator holds down a foot pedal outside the chamber. Take your foot off the pedal and the machine shuts down.

There was no way the operator could run the auger and also enter the chamber. Or so it seemed, but one enterprising employee found a way. He laid a heavy piece of metal on the foot pedal to keep the auger running while he entered the chamber to clear the ice jam. He was caught by the swirling auger and drawn inevitably, and fatally, into the ice machine.

Ironically, the employee had helped negotiate a labor contract stipulating that workers should scrupulously follow all safety procedures and abide by the company's operating rules.

Reference: *The Press*, Christchurch, New Zealand

DARWIN AWARD: PANCAKE THIEF
Unconfirmed by Darwin
JANUARY 2003, NEW DELHI, INDIA

Regarding accidental deaths during the construction of a subway, the *New York Times* wrote, "One of those killed was an unlucky thief who tried to steal braces holding up a concrete slab; it fell and killed him."

Reference: *New York Times*

DARWIN AWARD: ALL WOUND UP

Unconfirmed by Darwin

28 APRIL 2005, MOSCOW, RUSSIA

A construction worker drilling the foundation of a parking garage project on Starobitsevskaya Street noticed something shiny stuck to the swiftly rotating auger. He took a closer look but still couldn't identify the shiny object, so he reached down to grab it. Unfortunately, his jacket caught on the auger, winding his hand, his arm, and then his whole body into the apparatus. By the time his fellow workers could shut down the rig, "only the man's legs below the knees remained intact," according to the daily newspaper.

Reference: *Moskovskiy Komsomolets*

DARWIN AWARD: CATAPULT TO GLORY

Unconfirmed by Darwin
1987, MARGATE, ENGLAND

In 1987, the U.K. saw its most violent storm in three hundred fifty years. Winds exceeded ninety miles per hour, and an incredible amount of damage was done to property and people throughout the U.K. Millions of trees were uprooted by the hurricane-force gales.

In Margate in the county of Kent, one unfortunate homeowner had a property bordered by three massive poplars. The wind had felled one, which came to rest across his back garden. Another poplar had been bent over just far enough to lodge its top under the soffit of his roof. The foliage was blocking his upstairs bedroom windows; something had to be done.

This chap did not own a chain saw, nor could he reach the trunk of the tree from the house, even when leaning out the window. So he decided to shinny up and saw off the top while sitting astride the trunk, with his feet wedged against the gutter of his roof. He had plenty of time to reflect on the wisdom of his position, as it took him twenty minutes of sawing before the bent tree—which experts estimate held the energy equivalent to a small field gun—parted company with the portion trapped by the soffit, and sprang back upright.

Urban Legend? Many argue that the physics doesn't work; that there is no way a bent poplar has enough latent energy to rocket a human a distance of a mile. Although the distance the man supposedly traveled is inaccurate, the other details are plausible. It may be a true story with one exaggerated fact. We await confirmation.

His body was found in a neighbor's garden over a mile away. The police surgeon stated that his neck probably broke during the whiplash and he would blessedly have known nothing of the impact with the ground.

Reference: Various Margate newspapers in 1986

DARWIN AWARD: SIZZLING SCAFFOLDING

Unconfirmed by Darwin

1980S, TEXAS

At the town fairgrounds, some buildings were in need of a coat of paint, so local contractors were hired to do the job.

Between the buildings was an angled culvert, designed to drain rainwater away from the buildings. Because of the slope, the wheeled painter scaffolding tended to roll downhill, so the painters removed the wheels from the scaffolding. They were in the process of moving the scaffolding when the metal structure met a transformer. The painters were killed.

The story made the headlines. The town was abuzz with talk of the tragedy, how it had come to pass, and whether the city was liable for damages. The city officials decided they needed to conduct an investigation.

With much fanfare, they arrived at the scene of the incident, prepared to personally re-create the circumstances. Two officials grabbed the scaffolding in the exact same location as the two painters, began to move it . . . and were promptly electrocuted.

Reference: A Texas newspaper

READER COMMENTS:

"Stay tuned for the <u>next</u> investigation."

"Is there any way we can get all city, county, and state officials to investigate accidents in the same manner?"

HONORABLE MENTION: SERBIAN TSUNAMI
Unconfirmed by Darwin
26 DECEMBER 2004, SERBIA

Lucas, thirty, is the only known Serbian victim of the giant tsunami that devastated countries around the Indian Ocean. And he was at home in Serbia at the time. He blames television for the tragedy.

He was so shocked when he saw the tsunami footage on TV that he jumped out his apartment window. As he fell from the second floor, it occurred to him that the tsunami was not actually a threat to southern Serbia, which is separated by an entire continent from the Indian Ocean. But it was too late to avoid impact: He suffered two broken legs and a damaged spine.

Recovering later from his tsunami injuries, Lucas threatened to sue the local television station for announcing that "the tsunami is coming our way," and people should "immediately evacuate." A spokesperson for the television station said Lucas must have misunderstood the reporter's words.

Reference: 24ur.com

HONORABLE MENTION: HAMMER HEAD

Confirmed by Darwin

5 MARCH 2004, VICTORIA, AUSTRALIA

The construction trades have been revolutionized by new tools that are little short of miraculous. Take the nail gun. Operating on compressed air, it turns the tedious task of nailing into a simple point-and-click operation. It also makes possible a new way to injure yourself, one hitherto unknown: hammering a nail into your brain.

Stud, a thirty-three-year-old bricklayer, had just finished using a nail gun to install wall paneling at home. After the safety-minded man had turned off the compressor and removed the nail cartridge, he downed a few beers with his mates while they joked "about construction site accidents, and taking your eye out with a nail gun." For dramatic effect, Stud pointed his nail gun at his head and pulled the trigger. His mates noted a small red dot on his skin.

Stud figured the firing pin had simply glanced off his skull, powered by a leftover charge of compressed air. In fact, he had fired a 3.2-centimeter nail into his brain. He started to feel light-headed, but didn't feel much pain—due, perhaps, to the anesthetic effect of beer. Nevertheless, his son insisted on calling an ambulance.

When he arrived at the hospital the pain had become worse, so Stud asked the nurses for "a pair of pliers to pull it out myself." Instead, a neurosurgeon and a team of specialists spent four hours sawing through part of his skull and carefully removing the nail. Stud was expected to make a full recovery. "Luckily it lodged in the motor area of the brain and not a more critical area," said the doctor.

"I did a very stupid thing," said Stud. If the nail had been a centimeter deeper, he likely would have suffered permanent brain damage, or paralysis.

Reference: news.com.au, ananova.com, *Occupational Health & Safety Daily News*, Reuters

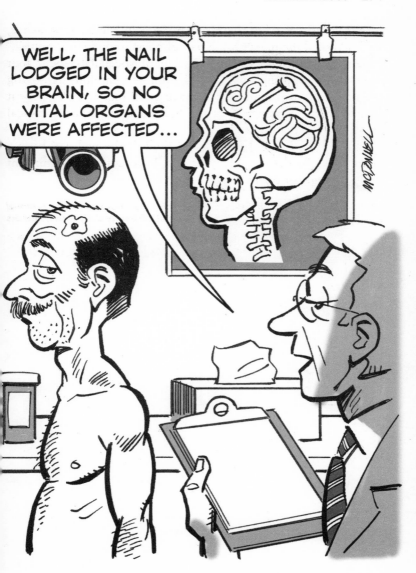

HONORABLE MENTION: OOPS, DID IT AGAIN
Confirmed by Darwin
31 JULY 2005, DARWIN, AUSTRALIA

A thirty-year-old resident of this aptly named town of sixty thousand, nestled in the Northern Territories on the Sea of Timor, just wanted to go home. But he was thwarted by two circumstances. First, he lived in an upper-level unit in a high-rise apartment building, and second, he had locked his keys in the apartment.

It was four A.M. Some people do their best thinking in the wee hours of the morning, but our protagonist was not one of them. He concluded that his best course of action was to scale the outside of the building. He managed to climb a short distance before he slipped.

Luckily, a parked car was beneath him to cushion the fall. He pulled himself off the shattered windshield and, unwilling to give up after one small setback, set out again to scale the wall. This time he reached the third floor before he slipped.

He was less fortunate than before, because he landed on his head, but also more fortunate, because this knocked him unconscious and saved him from a third attempt. He survived the fall, and was taken to Royal Darwin Hospital for treatment.

Lest outsiders get the wrong idea of Darwin, Australia, we include a comment from a sergeant on the Darwin police force: "It doesn't happen every day," he said.

Reference: *The Australian, Gold Coast Bulletin*

HONORABLE MENTION: WHITE RUSSIANS
Confirmed by Darwin
11 JUNE 2004, SIBERIA, RUSSIA

Khabarovsk is as far east as you can get in Siberia without falling into the Sea of Japan. It's home to military installations that conducted top-secret operations during the Cold War.

A few soldiers were poking around in the dump at their base and found a can full of a white powdery substance. At least twenty-five servicemen began using the handy substance, adding it to their tobacco when they rolled cigarettes, dusting it on their sweaty feet, and even snorting it. Within a short time, many of them became mysteriously ill and their hair began falling out.

Tests showed that the alluring white powder was thallium, an element once used as rat poison, but found to be so toxic that it is banned in the United States and several other countries. Extensive thallium exposure can cause liver and kidney damage, and organ failure.

Several soldiers were airlifted in serious condition to the St. Petersburg Academy of Military Medicine. They may not have earned a medal for their creative recycling efforts, but they did earn an Honorable Mention from the Darwin Awards.

Reference: BBC News, *Verdens Gang*

More about Thallium:

www.DarwinAwards.com/book/thallium.html

2003 PERSONAL ACCOUNT: ICARUS
Confirmed by Darwin
1911, FRANCE

"For sale cheap: one parachute used once, never opened."

I have a picture of someone who may be my relative, called Franz Reichelt. He is dressed in what looks like a huge black overcoat, and the caption reads, "Monsieur Franz Reichelt with his early parachute—an outstanding example of the way in which early aviators were as spectacular in their failures as in their successes.

"Reichelt was an Austrian tailor who sought to combine his interests by creating a garment to serve as both an overcoat and a parachute. In 1911, he decided to test his invention. Having told the authorities that he wanted to make a 'dummy' drop, at the last minute he strapped himself in, and with sublime confidence stepped from a platform off the Eiffel Tower, and fell to his death."

Reference: Personal Account; clipping of an unknown origin.

See a picture of Franz's overcoat!
www.DarwinAwards.com/book/icarus.html

Personal Account: Hot Hot Chocolate
1997, England

Unfortunately, I cannot confirm whether the following individual's ability to procreate was permanently impaired after this incident, but it certainly was for a while. . . .

I was chatting with a tradesman's apprentice whose boss was on a four-week leave of absence, claiming to have pulled a muscle in his leg. His customers complained mightily, as a backlog was piling up.

My friend—who shall, like his boss, remain nameless to protect his privacy—informed me of the *real* reason his boss was off work, a truth that he would not admit to his customers.

He had arranged a romantic weekend with his girlfriend, and had decided to spice up the evening with chocolate body paint. The instructions on the jar say to warm it in the microwave for a few seconds, but he misread the directions and microwaved it on high for two minutes.

You know how a mother tests baby milk on the back of her hand, to make sure it's not too hot? He didn't. He proceeded to pour the *very* hot chocolate onto his privates without realizing, until it made contact, exactly how hot it was. He suffered nasty burns, which gave him a John Wayne walk for weeks, and almost certainly put him out of sexual action for longer than that!

Reference: Personal Account

PERSONAL ACCOUNT: THE BIGGER THE BETTER
SEPTEMBER 2003, FLORIDA

A young man came into the emergency room complaining of scrotal pain. The triage nurse sent him to a waiting area, where his girlfriend held his hand lovingly and tried to comfort him. Two hours later he was called into an examination room. He insisted that his girlfriend wait outside. The male nurse who examined him saw that his scrotum had swollen to the size of a basketball, hanging down to his mid-thigh.

The nurse asked the young man how this had happened. After much hesitation, he finally confided that he attempted to make his scrotum appear larger to impress his girlfriend, who had remarked that he did not have "big balls" like her last boyfriend. He bought a kit online, and injected 500 cc of normal saline into his scrotum with an IV needle.

This self-improvement effort had caused a severe case of cellulitis, which required large doses of IV antibiotics and a three-day hospital stay. The doctor told him that the swelling had put tremendous pressure on his testes, and he might be sterile because of it.

He tried to hide his affliction from his girlfriend as he was moved upstairs to his room. The male nurse wasn't sure whether the young man had managed to impress her, but he had certainly proved to the ER staff that he had big balls.

Reference: Personal Account

PERSONAL ACCOUNT: CAPTAIN MAGNETO
SUMMER 2003, CANADA

During my days in the Canadian Air Force I worked at the gliding school instructing cadets. A magneto uses magnets to produce a powerful high-voltage electric current to fire the starters of an aircraft engine. One night we officers had a private competition to see who could hold onto the four leads of a magneto the longest. One by one we all dropped out, except for "Captain Magneto."

We pooled our money and came up with a bet, and the debonair Captain Magneto took the bet. He attached all four leads to his left testicle. Then we fired up the magneto. As you can imagine, Captain Magneto dropped like a sack of potatoes.

Nobody was able to assist him because we were all laughing too damn hard to breathe, let alone move. To add insult to injury, Mrs. Magneto (his wife) chose this very moment to walk in. She took one look at her husband, and instead of comforting him, started bitching him out. "What's wrong with you," she yelled, "I want kids someday!"

In time Captain Magneto was able to stand without screaming, but he probably won't be playing with magnetos anytime soon.

Reference: Personal Account

PERSONAL ACCOUNT: HUMAN PAPER TOWEL
APRIL 2003

Our office has a paper-towel dispenser in the kitchen. It holds a roll of blue paper towels, and towels are pulled from the center of the roll through a hole in the bottom of the dispenser. It is also refilled from the bottom. Press a catch and the base swings open, then a roll is shoved in, and the base is closed again. To prevent the roll from falling out before the base is closed, the dispenser is fitted with a "non-return device"—a set of plastic flaps that hinge up but not down.

Bill was bored. Computer programming wasn't sufficient exercise for his vivid imagination. He wandered into the kitchen to make some tea, and as he waited for the kettle to boil, his eye fell upon the towel dispenser. The cleaners had failed to refill it and it was empty, with its base hanging open.

Terminally bored, Bill felt a sudden urge to see what it looked like from the inside.

To his delight, his head fitted into the dispenser fairly well. He was not a particularly tall man, and the unit was mounted high on the wall, so he stood high on his tiptoes for a better view. That was just the right height. The non-return device "non-returned" right under his chin!

How long can one stand on one's tiptoes? Not very long, according to Bill's colleagues, who were attracted by the thrashing, choking noises coming from the kitchen. They found Bill dangling by the throat from a paper towel dispenser!

Fortunately, they were able to release him without permanent damage. It was quite entertaining to watch. I do wonder, however, what an inquest would have made of the situation if he *had* strangled himself.

And I wish I'd had a camera.

Reference: Personal Account

The perpetrator says, "OK, it was a daft idea, but hey, at least I know what the interior looks like. It was worth it."

READER COMMENT:

"I'll stick to photocopying my bum at work."

PERSONAL ACCOUNT: JUICE ME UP!
2005, FLORIDA

My cousin is a paramedic who related the following story to me. "Sparky" is a twenty-eight-year-old brand-spanking-new paramedic student. Today was his first day in the medic lab, and he marked this occasion by taking the defibrillator paddles, placing them on his chest and shouting, "Juice me up!"

Ding Dong Paramedic Student number two took him at his word, charging up the paddles and shocking Sparky at 360 joules. Sparky took all of six steps before collapsing and going into full cardiac arrest. His fellow classmates began CPR until the real paramedics arrived three minutes later. They defibrillated Sparky once again at 360 J, converting him into a normal sinus rhythm and saving his life. He was intubated, given one round of epi [epinephrin] and brought as a post-code to the emergency room where I work. With the hopes that Sparky did not sustain any brain damage from hypoxia, or ischemia to his heart, he should have a full recovery. I worked on Sparky for four hours tonight, eventually taking him to intensive care just before I left.

Sparky currently is a volunteer firefighter with aspirations of being hired as a paramedic/firefighter. In true EMS spirit, he has been given the new nicknames AC/DC and Joules, although his career in EMS is uncertain. He broke two golden rules:

1) If you don't know what it is, don't touch it.
2) If you know what it is, don't kill anyone with it.

The student that charged the defibrillator stayed after class to write, "I will not electrocute my classmates" one hundred times on the board.

Thank God for paramedics. And God, please protect children, fools, and paramedic students.

Reference: Personal Account

The End of the Universe

There's something seriously wrong with the universe!

To end the book, let us turn from the demise of the individual to the demise of the entire universe. Will it be Heat Death, the Big Crunch, or the Big Rip?

Stephen Darksyde, Science Writer

Long, long ago, in a galaxy far, far, away, a young star was paying the price for a life led too fast and too furious. The mighty sun had ripped through her precious store of hydrogen and briefly worked through the heavier elements until her nuclear furnace went dry; then she blew her starry guts out. The light of her destruction, now part funeral pyre and part grave marker, would thread its way past stellar nurseries and gaudy nebulae for over a hundred thousand years, until a small portion fell on the alien shores of a distant, blue-green planet circling a modest yellow star. There it would come to the attention of a recently evolved denizen that walked on two legs, known by the name of Colin Henshaw.

Prior to the day that violent supernova appeared in the sky, many mysteries of space and time were wrapped up in a pretty box called the Hot Inflationary Big Bang Model. The Big Bang explained why our cosmos is expanding; the Hot Inflationary Model covered how ripples of matter and energy arose in the infant universe to form the first galaxies and stars.

The looming question remaining in cosmology was how fast the universe is expanding, and whether it will end in fire or ice. If the mass of the universe is below a critical magnitude, it will keep expanding forever, and our cosmos will end in Heat Death: a perpetual state of utter black emptiness and cold. The background temperature will gradually approach absolute zero and such will be the fate of the cosmos to the grim end of time. If the mass of the universe is above that critical magnitude, one day it will stop expanding and slowly begin to contract. As the universe collapses, it will grow hotter and denser until time itself ends, and everything is contained in a single point known as a singularity: the Big Crunch. Both pictures are simple and compelling— and, as it turns out, wrong.

In the 1980s, cosmologists measured the universe's rate of expansion to a higher degree of accuracy than ever before. When they extrapolated the rate backward in time they ran into one hell of a paradox: The universe was younger than the oldest stars within it! It would be another decade before science would began to unravel this unwelcome twist. To understand how astronomers eventually made the biggest discovery since the Big Bang itself, let's return to that supernova.

On a balmy South African evening in 1987, our amateur astronomer noticed a tiny brilliant point in the Large Magellanic Cloud; one of two puffs of stars hanging high above the blazing disk of our own Milky Way galaxy. It hadn't been there before.

He called up a few observatories and asked them to check it out, certain that the professionals were already aware of the oddity. In that, he was wrong. Within hours of his report, though, every major observatory on Earth locked onto that region in the sky, to witness one of the most beautiful and destructive shows nature can put on. Supernova 1987A had arrived, the nearest to earth in a millennium.

Its legacy would shake the scientific community to its core.

One immediate benefit was that SN1987A demolished Young Earth Creationism, a belief that the universe was created only six thousand to ten thousand years ago. As seen with the eye of the mighty Hubble Space Telescope, the remnant of SN1987A is a single bright dot, surrounded by double offset rings of incandescent debris and a smaller primary ring centered on the core of what had once been the star. Because the apparent width of the ring can be measured, and because the actual diameter can be obtained using basic astrophysics, astronomers can directly calculate the distance to the supernova using simple trigonometry. That distance is 168,000 light-years. And scientists can categorically state that the light from SN1987A has not changed velocity during the transit. The conclusion is straightforward: She blew up 168,000 years ago, or about 160,000 years before Young Earth Creationists claim the universe existed.

But a more significant legacy of SN1987A would leave astronomers picking their collective jaw up off the floor. Observations of SN1987A led cosmologists to a new standard candle (an astronomical object with a known luminosity used to calculate distance) in a certain type of stellar remnant. The new technique allowed them to measure with unprecedented accuracy how fast galaxies are separating from one another. The results were astounding.

After meticulous observation to measure how fast the expansion of the universe was slowing down, the stunning conclusion was that the rate wasn't decreasing at all. The universe was expanding all right, but the rate of expansion was *increasing*. The universe was accelerating outward! The key to making the equations balance was a mysterious force dubbed "dark energy," which accounts for more than two-thirds of the mass of the entire cosmos. What we think of as "the universe"—stars, planets, light, atoms, and energy—is but a light frothing of what physicists call baryonic matter floating in an invisible sea of dark energy. And since this mysterious force is increasing in magnitude, if unchecked it will grow and grow, until galaxies, stars, planets, atoms, and even black holes are torn asunder: The Big Bang will end in the Big Rip!

Which brings us back to the puzzle of the universe being younger than the oldest stars within it. The formerly accepted estimate for the age of the universe was based on the false assumption that the expansion was slowing down. That age is a bit less than the new figure arrived at by assuming the rate of expansion is increasing. This explains the discrepancy between the age of the universe and the oldest stars within it. And although astronomers and physicists are now at an absolute loss to explain dark energy, at least the conundrum of old stars in a younger universe is cleared up.

Serendipity is waiting to strike again: The tantalizing clues into the nature of the dark-energy phenomena hint that, once resolved, the results will be as significant as when Isaac Newton was conked on the head with an apple.

References: Fact-checked with Dr. Sean Carroll,
Assistant Professor of Physics, University of Chicago

Appendices

WEBSITE BIOGRAPHY

The Darwin Awards archive was born on a Stanford University webserver in 1994. Its cynical view of the human species made it a favorite speaker in classrooms, offices, and pubs around the world. News of the website spread by word of mouth, and submissions flew in from far and wide. As the archive grew, so did its acclaim.

The website matriculated to its own domain in 1997, won dozens of Internet awards, and now ranks among the top 3,000 most-visited websites. It currently entertains half a million visitors per month in its comfortable Silicon Valley home. Guests are welcome to set off fireworks and play on the trampoline.

www.DarwinAwards.com is the locus for official Darwin Awards and related tales of misadventure. New accounts of terminal stupidity appear daily in the public Slush Pile. Visitors can vote on stories, sign up for a free email newsletter, and share their opinions on the Philosophy Forum—a community of free thinkers who enjoy numerous philosophical, political, and scientific conversations.

Some stories in this book include a URL directing you to a webpage with more information. All the hyperlinks can be explored starting from this portal:

www.DarwinAwards.com/book

AUTHOR BIOGRAPHIES

Wendy Northcutt studied molecular biology at Berkeley, worked in a neuroscience research laboratory at Stanford, and later joined a biotech startup developing treatments for cancer and diabetes. She wrote the Darwin Awards while waiting for her dastardly genetic manipulations to yield results.

Eventually Wendy shrugged aside lab responsibilities in favor of an offbeat career. She now works as a webmaster, and writes both code and prose for the Darwin Awards website. Much of her time is spent wishing she could catch up on work.

In her free time, Wendy chases eclipses, spends time with friends, and inhabits an increasingly eccentric wardrobe. Interests include reading, cooking, cats, gardening, and glassblowing. The vagaries of human behaviour continue to intrigue her.

Christopher M. Kelly is a writer and gifted Renaissance man. He graduated from Stanford University, worked at Apple Computer in Cupertino, and wrote a forthcoming biography about the man who invented the multivitamin, as well as the cult humor book *It's Okay to Be Happy,* in an attempt to cheer up a depressed girlfriend. Chris now lives in his hometown of Spokane, where he can be found scribbling in coffee shops, and participating in the Entrepreneurs Forum of the Great

Northwest (www.efgn.org). His current project is turning Spokane into an entrepreneurial Mecca.

Chris is in danger of winning a Darwin Award. He needs a muse and a mate. Chris seeks an attractive, intelligent, and kind woman to be his partner, his inspiration, and the mother of his offspring. Chris deserves to remain in the gene pool. Please don't let Chris's genes die out!

www.DarwinAwards.com/book/chris.html

BIOGRAPHIES OF CONTRIBUTORS

Annaliese Beery is a graduate student in neuroscience. Annaliese loves the entire field of biology, from molecular genetics to ecology. She spent several years teaching high school students AP biology, chemistry, computer science, and AP environmental science. While it's hard to beat summers off for field studies and outdoor adventures, Annaliese pried herself away from teaching and began her Ph.D. program a few years ago. She still collects biology stories of all kinds.

Annaliese contributed two essays:
"Love Bites," page 90.
"The Skinny on Fat," page 250.

Stephen Darksyde is a freelance science writer with a strong background in math and physics. He has a longstanding interest in conveying the wonder and importance of science to the layperson. Stephen writes regularly for the *Daily Kos*, one of the most visited blogs in the world. He lives near Kennedy Space Center in Florida in "Darksyde Manor" with Mrs. DS, a cat named Nikki, and a dog named Darwin.

Stephen contributed four essays:
"AIDS, Bubonic Plague, and Human Evolution," page 26
"Aquatic Apes Are People, Too!," page 66
"Endogenous Retroviruses and Evolution," page 150
"The End of the Universe," page 283.

Peter McDonnell is a freelance illustrator who has been creating pop art, comic book, and cartoon illustrations for a long list of national clients for over twenty years. After living and working in the beautiful-but-foggy city of San Francisco since 1981, he and his wife Shannon packed up their baby boy, Jacob, and their respective studios, and moved to the sunny town of Petaluma, forty miles north of the Golden Gate Bridge. Explore Peter's work at www.mcdonnellillustration.com.

James G. Petropoulos was born and raised in Queens, New York City. He attended Fordham Preparatory School in the Bronx and Northwestern University in Evanston, Illinois (BA, Naval Commission). James works as an animator and director in traditional drawn media and CGI. He served as a Naval Reserve officer for eleven years and is now a bandsman with the 199th Army Band, NY Army National Guard. He is a professional bandleader and jazz percussionist, as well as a Sunday School teacher, Freemason, and Darwin Awards moderator.

James contributed the essay,
"Brother, Can You Spare a Banana?" on page 118.

Scientist Tom Schneider studies the mathematics of biology. "Living things are too beautiful for there not to be a mathematics that describes them." He spends his free time on the contra dance floor, and cohabits with a cactus named Hairy who has not yet participated in pasta experiments.

Tom contributed the parody scientific research paper, "Origin of the Novel Species *Noodleous doubleous*," page 17.

Norm Sleep teaches geophysics at Stanford University. His interests include conditions on the Earth and the habitability of other planets. He was born in Kalamazoo, Michigan, and grew up in the paper mill town of Parchment. He graduated from Michigan State University and arrived at MIT during the plate tectonic scientific revolution. His thesis was on subducting slabs. He taught at Northwestern University before moving to Stanford. His interest in habitability stems from his work on hydrothermal circulation at midoceanic ridges and his work on the feeble tectonic activity on Mars.

Norm contributed the essay,
"Chicken Little Was Right," on page 182.

Maia Smith will not be returning to school this fall. Instead, she plans to travel full-time, returning to Martha's Vineyard each summer to work, hang out with friends, and decompress. Her list of possible careers includes any combination of midwife, bush pilot, artist, commercial diver, overseas English teacher, ethicist, and satirist; for now, "professional vagrant" seems apt. Her most recent travels are chronicled on her website, www.maiasadventures.com.

Maia contributed the essay,
"Forensic Analysis: Achieving Justice," on page 226.

Location Index

Story Index